A VINEYARD OF FERVOR

LYRICS OF LOVE

FRANK VINCENT CASALE

A VINEYARD OF FERVOR
LYRICS OF LOVE

iUniverse books may be ordered through booksellers or by contacting:

iUniverse
1663 Liberty Drive
Bloomington, IN 47403
www.iuniverse.com
844-349-9409

Because of the dynamic nature of the Internet, any web addresses or links contained in this book may have changed since publication and may no longer be valid. The views expressed in this work are solely those of the author and do not necessarily reflect the views of the publisher, and the publisher hereby disclaims any responsibility for them.

Any people depicted in stock imagery provided by Getty Images are models, and such images are being used for illustrative purposes only.
Certain stock imagery © Getty Images.

ISBN: 978-1-6632-4427-7 (sc)
ISBN: 978-1-6632-4426-0 (e)

Library of Congress Control Number: 2022915509

Print information available on the last page.

iUniverse rev. date: 10/25/2022

I dedicate this book to my lovely wife,
Pamela.

CONTENTS

INAMORATA

For years, I have wept blue devils.
A silent murmur of loneliness and hunger
So excruciating that the tears of sorrow
Have scarred the face of my soul with tears of blood.
In darkness, I have wandered,
A lost soul in a void of emptiness,
Feeling the cold arms of nothingness surround me as I blindly searched
for love.

Imprisoned in a realm of black,
Its walls slowly closing in around my aching heart,
Crushing my hopes and dreams of ever finding a true lover
Until I myself have become absorbed into nothingness.
Painfully I have starved for the love and passion of a woman,
A woman whom I could join in holy matrimony,
Where our hearts would melt together and our souls become vessels of
divine intimacy,
Sharing the tender mercies of our deepest emotions and desires,
Mixing our love into one,
Becoming an endless ocean of passion
Filled with devotion and faithfulness,
Being completely balanced in absolute equality.

Trapped in the seclusion of despair,
I have lived for years in constant craving,

A churning appetite of immeasurable depth,
My heart an open abyss
That appeared to be incapable of ever being filled,
For the more I hungered to love and be loved,
The greater my pain deepened,
To the point that I truly believed
The grave would swallow me into its earthly body
Where my soul would be digested into eternal loneliness,
Never ever knowing the identity of my true love.
Then one special day, everything just changed.
Like the kaleidoscope from one phase to another,
You appeared before my eyes,
Piercing the darkness with your colors of love:
Colors of warmth and sensitivity,
Colors of compassion and understanding,
Colors of purity and integrity—
Colors of such passion that your eyes glistened a rainbow of incandescence
Where, at its end, lies the living treasure of your heart and soul and
Your love, your sweet unconditional love.
You stood before me lustrous as the moon,
Blissfully bright across the starlit night—
A luminous figure set in heavens blue,
Full of energy and wonder.
Your ardent rays pierced through my heart
Like arrows from Cupid's bow,
Beautiful and delicate as a rose
Naked in essence, yet dressed in its own garment of elegance,
Fully bloomed and oozing with seductiveness—
A silent sexuality that speaks vigorously without words.

Your beauty so overwhelming that I believed you were nothing more than
an illusion—
Just a passing perception within my mind,
A mirage of such loveliness and splendor
That you would fade away from me the moment I would reach for you,

Afraid to move in your direction for fear you would vanish from my vision,
So I kept myself at a safe distance,
Silently loving you within my heart.
I felt it was better to love you from a distance
And have the presence of your beauty in my life
Than to reach for you and be cast back into the darkness I came from,
Where the sight of your loveliness would be lost forever.

For quite some time, fear kept me at length;
The unseen leash around my soul
Would yank me violently at the mere thought of even getting closer to you.
Like a choker, fear was the grisly necklace locked around my heart;
The more I yearned for you, the tighter fear got,
Its vise-like grip trying to strangle the love I have for you to death.
But my passion refused to be extinguished;
It only intensified like a cutting torch,
White flames of love blazed,
Burned, burned, burned, their way through the chains,
Freeing me from the bondage of fear.

From chains of fear to chains of love:
I have become your prisoner of passion.
Locked in love's tender embrace,
Our bodies absorb the emotional vibes of desire,
Flowing from heart to heart, an internal conversation between our souls.
Into your dark eyes I deeply stare,
Seeing the mystic garden within your heart:
An exotic vineyard of zaftig grapes,
Oozing with ebullient juices of erotic flavors;
Your eccentric love is the very nectar of your soul—
A love as astronomical as the heavenly stars.

But it was not until I kissed your lips
That I tasted the sweet revelation of you,
Realizing you were no longer an illusion within my mind

But the very reality I pined for all of my life:
My one and only true love,
My deepest dream came true.
Inamorata, my beautiful inamorata,
I will devote the rest of my life to loving you.

MORNING BLISS

The morning sun gently beams across our bed,
Its comforting rays seep through the curtains,
Lightly kissing our faces good morning.

Slowly I awake to the delicate music of birds
Singing their morning songs of praise.
Snuggled against my chest your lovely face sleeps in tranquility
As the sun shines across your nakedness, highlighting the beauty of you.

I deeply stare at you,
Overwhelmed and awed by the sight of your celestial radiance.
Slowly I touch you, bringing my hands to your ravishing hair
That flows like a dark river down the arch of your back.
My fingers swim freely up stream through black strands of soft waves,
Reaching the ivory shores of your brow;
My fingertips walk gracefully over the seashells of your closed eyes,
Crossing the bridge of your refined structured nose,
Down to the folds of your succulent lips.
Gently I trace the fullness of your mouth,
My finger skates round and round the softness of your lips;
Sliding down the smoothness of your jaw, I cup your chin—
I lean over to kiss you.

First kiss of the day:
Our lips lock in morning passion,
Welcoming one another deeply,
Our tongues embrace with hunger.
Slowly your eyes open as our lips gently part.
I'm drawn into your dark, loving eyes,
Completely lost in the wonders of you.

The sight of you is delightful,
As the sun shines its light upon you
A gardenia of ardent fire, full of desire,
Your skin, soft as petals,
Silky, milky, and warm
Your beauty, such great beauty
Immensely excites me.

Drawn to you like a bumblebee that pollinates,
Sucking the nectar from its flower,
My mouth thirsts for you,
To taste the sweetness of your breasts.
Your aroma intoxicates me;
Your flesh I cannot resist.
I pull you closer to me.
Skin to skin, our bodies copulate in the affinity of love,
Linked and locked in burning passion—
Body, soul, heart, and mind
Enveloped together as one flesh
In the divine state of morning bliss.

SAFE LOVE

The heart is the foundation of a true relationship.
It's constructed for giving, love, kindness, and warmth,
Built for the security of someone's love and trust,
Knowing there is safety in that person.
I have found that safety in you,
A place where I can rest assured that my love will not be taken for granted,
Or my heart be wounded by lies and meaningless words of love.
Because of you, I believe in love again;
I have faith in you immensely.

You have proven to me in countless ways that your heart is real
And that your love for me is absolute.
There are no flaws in you;
You are everything I ever dreamed of and so much more.
You are perfect to me because you are yourself:
Beautiful and wonderful—
And I love you just the way you are.

Your heart is a place of security,
A vault for my love,
And I'm deeply satisfied with you,
So do not ever change your combination,
Because I have found my peace in you.

Safe love, insured by the integrity of a pure heart,
Strongly protected by a firm code of fidelity
Because of the soul's completeness in God's law and decrees, we are one.

Your heart and soul are sound in all their ways,
Full of honor, truth, and faithfulness.
I give all my love to you in trust, without fear or regret,
Undoubtedly knowing that the love I have for you
Is treasured, respected, and safe forever within your heart.
My love is yours.

DEFINITION OF LOVE

You are the definition of love.
Without you, there is no meaning.
Love is fulfilled by your actions.
The essence of the word is your true character.

Ever since we first met, you have surrounded my life with love;
Everything you say and do fills my heart with overwhelming passion,
From a wink of your eye, to our first kiss,
I have felt the force of your love,
From a whisper to a touch,
A smile to an embrace,
I have received the love of you.

Love pours out of you like the redness of a rose;
Its awesome power of attraction intoxicates me deeply,
Stimulating my heart and soul with the silent loudness of its aura,
Elevating my senses to higher levels of consciousness,
Enhancing my vision and taking me to a place of clarity,
Where my heart, soul, and mind absorb the nakedness of love's purity.

Seeing love's elegant figure exotically dance in the depths of your fire-lit eyes,
Tasting the deliciousness of love's secret nectar upon your succulent lips,
Hearing love's fervent voice speak to me through the fluttering of your heart's tongue,

Feeling love's emphatic hands erotically caress me through the softness of
your fingertips,
And smelling love's heavenly fragrance in the warmth of your sweet breath.

You are love; love is you.
You define the meaning to the fullest description;
Without obstruction of its truth or distortion of its justice,
You live out the reality of love,
Proving the beauty of its very existence in everything you say and do.
You are always and forever my true love.

SKETCHES

Sketches of you fill my mind,
Graphic as life itself,
Each turning page more vivid than the last—
Takes me back, way back to the days of our love,
When our hearts were in unison
And being with you was the sweetest elation I ever experienced.

Just the mere sight of your beauty enchants my soul to silent tears.
From the first time I saw your exotic features, my heart was yours.
You are the essence of beauty, ultimate beauty;
Out from the isles of heaven you appeared before me:
Empyrean, lovely, awesome—
A human sculpture of divinity.
You are beautiful, extremely beautiful.

On the wings of sweet desire,
Into one another's hearts we flew.
Like lovebirds on a branch singing ballads of true romance,
Our hearts chirped with love, affection, admiration.
Our love soared as high as the constellations
And dove as deep as the abyssal blue.
Within the grips of my memory, I have cherished these moments of you.

From the first time I held your hands in mine, I felt the warmth of your heart.
Looking deeply into your eyes, I saw roses of love—

Supreme love—red, red roses eternal.
To those quiet evenings we spent at home cuddling to candlelight, soft jazz, and fine wine,
From the first time I tasted your lips and became completely addicted to the fruit of your
amorous kisses,
To those heart-to-heart talks with tears flowing freely to the rhythm of emotions,
From those midnight drives down starlit highways feeling exuberant and pink,
To those moonstruck picnics by the bridge side,
From the walks in the rain to dancing in the park,
From playing in the snow to lying in the sand—
Always together regardless of weather,
You and me hand in hand.

I remember the first time we made love.
Slowly we undressed each other as if unwrapping some long-awaited gift.
Your nakedness hypnotized me, each curve of your figure stimulated my whole being.
I can still smell the fragrance of your lush hair, and feel the silkiness of your creamy
Skin.
I can still see us intimately locked together,
Erotically exploring our passions,
Opening the gates of our innermost recesses without fear, doubt, or regret.

Those precious times that we shared have never faded away.
These sketches of you are forever preserved on the canvas of my heart,
Freshly painted and brighter than ever.
I deeply yearn for you, to return to sacred place and time
When our passions blissfully burned in the arms of love's true embrace.
I miss you. I miss you ineffably.
Behind a cascade of tears, these old embers have never died;

They have remained aglow all this time, softly burning sweet memories of you.
Within the sanctuary of my heart, a choir of songbirds still sings hymns to your name;
I never lost my love for you.
You are forever my soulmate.
Neither time nor distance will ever erase these sketches of you.

TO CATCH A DREAM

Last night I was thinking of you
So deeply, that I cried myself to sleep,
And within my mind,
I elevated the thought of being with you
So hard that I rose from my bed
And left my body as my spirit fled.

At my bedside staring down at myself,
My body still and vacant,
Lost in a dark, soundless dormancy,
Physically unaware of my own absence,
I left my body where it lay
And walked off into the night,
Silent and unseen,
With the strong intention of catching a dream.

Into the evening, I drifted
Swiftly, smoothly, and undisturbed,
Dancing across the land in a ghostly balletic rhythm
Through rich spicy gardens,
Maneuvering through dark, woody pines
And as I glided across the green grassy dew,
My feet remained dry as I searched for you.

I threw my hands up to the moon
And slowly I ascended,
Vaulting above the stars;
In constant awareness
I absorbed everything across the blue
As I continued my voyage to you.

Soaring the skies high above the mountain peaks,
I hovered on a current of air
Then dove rapidly toward the sea,
Lightly touching the ocean's waves.
I stretched myself upward into the winds,
Reaching the stars so bright,
Then flew off into the moonlit night.

Instinct told me I was close, my awareness alive, senses keen.
I focused on a city of lights, circling round and round,
Until I found your town
Then slowly I descended to the ground.
In front of your house I stood,
Staring up at your window.
Then I walked to your door, passing through with ease.
Inside I searched for you.
I found your room and entered.
Beside your bed, I watched you sleep,
Then I bowed my head and began to weep.

Tears of passion in my eyes
Slowly rolled down my cheek
I sat by your side and whispered "I love you"
As the moon glowed on your sleeping face,
Your mouth slightly parted, inhaling dreams.
Gently I caressed your dark lovely hair.
You never knew that I was there.

I cradled you in my arms, feeling the warmth of your breasts.
I listened to the evenness of your breathing
As your heart slowly pumped sweet blood through your veins.
I pressed my lips against your ear, and softly spoke words of love,
Expressing my emotions from the depths of my heart to the core of my soul
Where my love constantly yearns
And my passion forever burns.

To catch my dream, I had to travel through my sleep
Just to be with you,
Because I needed to see you, to hold you, to say "I love you."
Distance will never keep me from you
For my love is an endless chain
Linked and locked to your heart forever.
As long as I can dream, and picture you within my mind,
I'll find your destination, always be able to come to you
Just to give you a good night kiss.
Through dreaming I've captured this sweet bliss.

DISTANT LOVERS

No matter how distant we are,
The miles never come between us
Because our love is strong and sincere.
We share a mystical closeness
Deep within our hearts
That no distance can ever break.

Even though we are very far apart
And the time between us seems forever,
I never feel alone
Because whenever I close my eyes,
I see your beautiful face,
And hear your voice so sweetly whisper
"I love you," in the core of my heart.

I feel the warmth of your soul
Cuddle close to mine,
Gently embracing my emotions
With your love and tenderness.
You are within my heart and soul, always soothing the pain of missing you.

My love for you is faithfully yours,
And there is no distance or time that can ever change my heart.
You are my soulmate.
The closeness and the bond of our love is eternal.

SMOTHER ME

Comfort me always
With your heart and soul;
Embrace me tightly
And never let me go.
Surround me with your presence
So I'm never alone;
Blanket me with your emotions
So I'll never get cold.

Envelop me with tender care
In my times of sickness;
Shelter me with concern
And keep me safe.
Enclose me with gentleness
When I'm full of sorrow;
Lavish me with kindness
So I know you understand.

Intoxicate me with words
So I know your heart;
Entangle me with actions
So I know your loving ways.
Reinforce me with strength
When I'm feeling weak and weary;
Cover me with your sweetness
So that I never turn bitter.

Drown me with kisses
From your lips of affection;
Consume me with caresses
So I never forget your touch.
Suffocate me, my darling, I don't mind.
Smother me with all your good intentions,
And never ever let me go,
For your love it keeps my heart alive.

REMINISCING

Yesterday's memories
Soar through my consciousness,
Each vision crystal-like
Within the mind's eye.
Your face appears before me;
Seeing your beauty captivates my sight—
Remembrance so vigorous
It seems as if it is a reality.

The soft tone of your voice
Echoes whispers of love;
Listening to each word you speak,
My ears embrace the sounds of bliss.
Smelling your loving scent,
Absolute and sweet,
Your essence clouds my thoughts,
Leaving my mind in a pleasant state.

Your fingers gently brush my brow,
Searching for the hidden face
That lies beyond these eyes of green.
Feeling your tender caresses,
My skin absorbs your touch
Sending emotional currents through my flesh.

Lips lightly locked
As our tongues passionately buss,
Tasting one another hungrily.
Our souls become ringed
Forever within our hearts.
O God, how I wish you were here.

HUNGER

Passion, an inferno of love,
Its flames burn endlessly within me.
My heart cries out your name,
Over and over with every beat;
Its bloody tears never end.

The loneliness never ceases.
My body hurts with desire—
Yearning, yearning to be with you.
I need to touch your skin,
To caress the softness,
To lightly lick every pore,
Tasting the sweetness of your existence.

Come press your lips upon mine;
Comfort me with kisses.
Let our tongues gently embrace,
Exploring one another's mouths.
I pine deeply for your love.
Quench my thirst with your saliva
For its flavor is the essence of your heart.

My love for you is fire—
A fire called hunger.

Blood travels my veins like lava,
My body a volcano, my heart a torch—
A flame that can never be extinguished.
I'm hungry, hungry for you.
My hunger is endless,
Like a wild beast who eats and eats
Yet still seeks for food,
His appetite was never satisfied.
My fire roars like a lion
Who prowls the jungle in heat
In search of his queen.

Famished my heart, delirious my mind—
My hunger is uncontrollable.
Let me coil myself around you.
Feel the warmth of my passion
As I envelop you in my arms
And devour you with kisses

Let me lightly buss your belly,
Feast off your breasts, neck, and ears;
Let me drown myself in your eyes:
Those pools of passion where I may swim freely within your heart.

Feed me, feed me your love,
For my heart pulsates hunger—
Hunger is endless for you.
I'm starving for your flesh
Like a wolf starves for his prey;
I crave for your heart
Like he craves for blood;
I pine to sing out your name
With a vociferous force of rapture,
Like his howls at the moon
Echo through the valleys.

I'm a lone wolf without a pack
In a forest of loneliness;
My heart, a wolf's cave,
Desperately lonely.
My only company is my hunger,
Which keeps me strong, alive, and in love.
I love you more than lips can speak.
I hunger you, only you.
I love you.

FULFILLMENT OF LOVE

I have opened up the doors to my heart and soul for you,
And like a river you have flowed into me,
Filling my heart with the absoluteness of your love,
And the waves of your affection current throughout my body.
I give to you the innermost recesses of my spiritual being.
And all the thoughts within my mind have been channeled into you.
You've become my main focus in life,
For you have given my heart tranquility,
And my soul the warmth of a summer breeze
Blowing softly through wind chimes.
Love has been fulfilled by your actions.
The essence of the word is your character,
For you are the definition of true love,
And without you there's no meaning.
Beyond your facade, I see your true self.
You are more than every woman can ever be
And greater than all the ladies that are;
You are the fulfillment of agape love.

WHEN WE FIGHT

Every time we fight,
I feel lost and lonely,
My body hollow and cold
Like a seashell
Left on some deserted beach
To be washed away.

Every time we fight,
I feel weary and dazed,
My mind clouded
As a damp dreary day
That's grey and meaningless
And never seems to end.

Every time we fight,
I feel pain and sorrow,
My heart carbon-paper blue
As the black evening sky,
Silently crying
Throughout the starless night.

Every time we fight,
I feel bleak and melancholy,
My soul full of misery,
Like the clown with a painted smile;
He performs before many
But he himself cannot laugh.

DIFFERENCES

I know there are times
We don't see each other so clearly;
Our eyes become out of focus
And our moods run wild,
To the point
That we fall into the state of emotional discomfort,
Leaving us completely melancholy.

But in those times of disagreements,
Misunderstandings, and differences
Is when we become closer,
Because those are the times
When we learn about our identities in each other,
And grow more aware and sensitive
Of one another's deepest emotions,
Thoughts, and beliefs.

In those times of controversy,
We build new foundations
And strengthen our relationship
With support and reinforcement
Of the heart and soul,
Bring our love
Back into balance.

UNDYING EMOTION

My heart, a fireplace of love,
The inner mounting flames
Grow wildly with each passing day,
The temperature rising beyond degrees of reading,
A roaring fire of pure desire,
An endless passion pulsating for you.

My blood, a river of lava,
Constantly flowing my veins with absolute love;
Each blood cell knows your name,
And with every passion and desire that I have for you
Burns an eternal flame in the deepest recesses of my being.
My soul, a blood-red spiritual sea
Full of incandescent bliss,
Intense with love, devotion, and integrity,
Forever for you.

You, my darling, a precious ship
That I have allowed to enter my waters;
Sail wherever you may please,
Explore freely the depths of my soul,
Lose yourself in my quiet storm of love,
For I welcome you with waves of undying emotion.

So come dive into my ocean,
Swim within my tears;
Let me drown you with my love,
For my passion is everlasting
And my love for you a hunger that knows no death.

RHYTHM

My heart powerfully pulsates
Never-ending desire for you.
The rhythm of my heart
Pumps ardent currents of love
Through my palpitating arteries;
Each contraction generates waves of emotion
That flow through my system
In rapid beats of ignited passion.
Each throb thrusts through my veins
Fiery heart-shaped blood cells that dance and sing
To the rhythmical vibrations
Of my soul-drumming heart.

My soul synthesizes songs
That I sincerely feel for you;
Every lyric that I write
Is arranged in sequence
To the various percussions of my heart.
Every energized emotion
Is played for you in perfect harmony
To the instrumental expressions
Of my inner-most being.
Each snare, bass, and parade
Romantically beats for you,
The absolute essence of my love
Ending every song
With passionate kisses of my cymbals.

UNCOMMON LOVE

It took some time
To roll the stone over
And see what was on the other side.
No matter how hard I struggled,
I never gave up on you.
It was worth the effort
To find the love you tried to hide.
I knew in my heart
That deep inside of you
Was a special love
Which you never revealed
To anyone else before.
I knew if I got inside of your heart
You'd be my lady forever,
So I used my love to open your door.

My love for you would not surrender
Because I wanted you so deeply.
So I fought my way through your wall of ice,
Melting my way into your heart
With the passions of my inner flame,
Seeping my way into your soul
So I could give you my love
And take away your pain.
I never gave up on you;

My love for you would not allow it.
I would have walked through fire
To give you my heart.
I would have given up my life
To save yours.
I would have sold my soul
To be your eternal lover.

My love for you is endless,
Pure, faithful, and uncommon.
The depths of my passion go beyond time
And now that you're mine,
My lovely lover,
I will never let you go,
For my love will live
Long after death.

When I fell in love with you,
I saw the passion burning in your eyes,
And I knew you loved me too.
Even though you gave me one long-distance race,
You were worth the chase.
My heart endured every trial and test you threw my way,
And my love for you prevailed.

For those who said they loved you
Then gave up on you
Did not love you enough
To suffer the pain,
Or even try.
Their loss was my gain.
For I wanted you so badly
That I would have fought the Devil himself
To win your love.
In my arms you belong,

Where my love will always flow
From my heart to yours,
Never ever letting you go.
Behind my eyes of green
There are tears of endless love,
Greater in number than the stars.
All my love I give to you.
I place my heart in your hands.

TOTAL DARKNESS

Somehow we have fallen
And our hands became separated,
Leaving me in total darkness,
Broken and alone.
My soul crawls blindly.
On my hands and knees,
I search for you,
But you're nowhere to be found.
I call your name
But receive no answer.
The cold silence has seeped into my soul,
Making me numb and weary.
I must find you.

A black blanket from hell
Has covered me once again,
Leaving me in an ocean of darkness,
Loneliness, and despair.
I must find your hand
Before we drown.
Where are you?
Without you in my life
There is no light;
I'm just a candle without its flame,
My tears frozen still
Like streaks of dried wax.

I need you always
To see, hear, smell, to taste, and feel.
I need you in my life
To kiss, to love; to live
Without you, there is no warmth,
No passion, no desire.
I yearn for no other
For you are my one and only
True fire.
Without you there is only emptiness—
Just a black, cold void within my heart.
Without you there is no peace,
No balance, no life.
I must find you—find you soon,
For without you I'm nothing, nothing at all—
Total darkness.

HARSH WORDS

I sit in lonely silence,
Feeling the painful sorrow of my broken heart
As I violently weep over you
Fat, fat tears,
Waterfall from my eyes,
As sweet and sour thoughts
Drift through my mind,
Trying to understand
What went wrong between us.

Harsh words spoken
In an angry rush;
Two hearts broken,
Feelings crushed;
Fiery tongues dueling,
Lover against lover—
Foolish, foolish us
To speak jagged words to each other.
We've been together for many years
Far too long to howl at one another
With fire, fury, and fangs
As if we were enemies.

In a stormy heart's rage,
Mouths full of thunder
Speak lightning words,
Causing painful wounds
That last a lot longer
Than the moment's anger.
Harsh words spoken
In an angry rush,
Two hearts now broken,
Feelings crushed;
Piercing words of bitterness,
Vociferous and keen.
We should know better than to speak irate words
That our hearts really don't mean.

MOONSTRUCK MELODY

My mind often drifts back to that cool evening when we first met.
I have taken that sacred night and stored it within the inner chambers of
my soul,
Where I may draw upon its precious memory at will
So that I can reflect and relive its joyful experience over and over again,
For that evening was the greatest evening of my life,
And I will deeply cherish it for as long as I live.

I remember that night as if it were yesterday:
The moon was a swollen orb of ghostly splendor
Surrounded by a cerulean veil of starlight.
Heavy vibes filled the atmosphere
As I walked aimless through the city streets,
Feeling melancholy and insomniac—
My heart ached with bitter loneliness.
I yearned for a woman.
I craved for a lover.
I hungered for love:
True love,
Free love,
Endless love.

Somewhere in the midnight sky, the stars began to dance
To the music of a celestial ensemble
Conducted by the hands of God;

Its melodic sound magically lured us together.
Out from the heavens and into my heart
You flew into my life like a sylph in white.
At first I thought you were just a sweet apparition,
Some moonlight mirage,
It wasn't until we stood face to face that I realized you were no illusion.

The moon reflected within your eyes like pearls of fire.
Ardent passion poured from you with great force,
Its vibrant rays pierced through my heart like bolts of lightning.
Moonstruck with desire,
I was captivated by your beauty;
Never have I seen a lady as luscious as your self.
Your exoticness enchanted my soul,
Overwhelming me with sweet emotions.
Love emerged from my heart as red as fresh-bloomed roses.

Something mystical occurred that night—
Something so wonderful that it changed my life forever.
Love struck the inner chords of my heart
Like a master harpist;
Unseen fingers fervently played the most hypnotic melodies.
Each composition flowed freely
With love, devotion, and surrender.
Unrestrained emotions, emancipated bliss—
A storm of fiery tears arose from the depths of my soul,
Pouring with romantic intensity,
Oozing with poetic urgency,
Wanting you,
Needing you,
Loving you and only you
Because there is no one else like you.
You are my moonlight lover.
You are the melody of my heart.
You are forever the song of my soul.

FOREVER YOURS

My blood flows through me with unfading love for you.
You're always with me,
In heart and soul.
You're constantly on my mind throughout the day,
And endlessly within my dreams throughout the night.
My heart belongs to only you.
I'm forever yours for all ages to come.

The love I have for you is endless
Because you're the precious rose
That has pierced through my heart
And the center of my life.
I'll always love and care for you.
For all eternity
I'll attend to all your needs and wildest desires.

Being faithfully yours throughout our lifetime,
Treasuring you
In the depths of my being,
My heart, soul, and love for you
Will always remain
Everlasting and imperishable.
I'm forever yours.

EXCLUSIVELY MADE

She came into my life
Like a fallen autumn leaf
And landed upon my lap with a silent loudness.
Full of crisp color and uniqueness,
She is what she is:
She's a splendid autumn leaf
Exclusively made just for me.

She came into my life
Like a doe from some celestial forest
And drifted onto my path with delicacy.
Full of purity and innocence,
She is what she is:
She's a divine doe
Exclusively made just for me.

She came into my life
Like a fresh bloomed red rose
And enkindled my environment with a sweet essence.
Full of veracious love and individuality,
She is what she is:
She's a radiant rose
Exclusively made just for me.

She came into my life
Like a swan across a pond
And swam into my heart with grace,
Full of beauty and elegance.
She is what she is:
She's an exquisite swan
Exclusively made just for me.

She came into my life
Like a lovebird from an island of paradise
And flew into my soul with blissful songs,
Full of passion and desire.
She is what she is:
She's a gorgeous love-bird
Exclusively made just for me.

She came into my life
Like a woman of sovereignty, a lady, a lover,
And filled my lonely world with all of her excellent qualities.
Full of intensity, integrity, and intimacy,
She is what she is:
She's a magnificent woman, enchanting lady, and ultimate lover
Exclusively made just for me.

She came into my life
Like a precious jewel
And changed the value of my life for the better.
Full of richness, and sacredness,
She is what she is:
She's my beautiful lovely jewel
Exclusively made just for me.

THINKING OF YOU

From the moment I open my eyes
Until I go to sleep again,
Thoughts of you flood my mind
Like a rapid river flows
Over rocks and waterfalls,
Steady, without pause
To an ocean of vivid consciousness
Where I think of you with absolute clarity,
Losing myself on waves of vivacious visions
And drowning myself in the depths of dreams
Where I'm surrounded by the beauty of your existence.

Asleep or awake,
You're constantly on my mind.
Dream state—such a wonderful state,
Whether it's day or night,
I'm thinking of you,
Each thought an encounter of ecstasy
That fills my heart and soul
With such bliss and tranquility
That I experience each and every thought of you
Just as if it was the present reality.

FOREVER LOVE

Forever love,
My heart swells at the sight of you,
Bulges to maximum,
Flooding my blood vessels with celestial passion
That blazes throughout my body
In flames of cosmic incandescence.
My desire increases with each encounter,
Rising higher and higher,
Blinding my eyes to everything that's around me
Except for you—
Beautiful, beautiful you.

Into your eyes I fall—
Those dark lovely eyes
Full of depth and story
That always mystically comfort me
With sweet silent kisses.
Your beauty takes me away, far, far away
To that wonderful place of enchantment
That lies deep inside of you
Where there is only love,
Absolute love, your love—
Forever love.

I'LL DIE FOR YOU

You mean more to me than the world's riches.
Without you, my life is meaningless.
And I would lay down my life for you
In a heartbeat,
For your life is more precious to me than mine.
You have much more to offer this earth
Then I would in ten lifetimes.
I would dive head first into my grave
Before I would allow death to take you away.
The mere thought of death's boney fingers touching your pretty heart
And squeezing the life out of you frightens me.

I would take any death in your place,
From the worst of tragedies to any diseases.
I'd rather die twice
Then see you die once.
Let me die painfully
So that you don't have to suffer at all.
I would rather give up my place in heaven
Then to see you die before me.
God knows this.
So let it be that I die first.
Let your death fall upon me
In exchange for your life

So that you may live your life to the fullest:
Healthy, happy, and free
Joining me at a far more later age,
Softly in your dreams filled with peace and wonder—
No pain, no suffering, no tragedy—
Only absolute love, only ultimate bliss,
Where you'll rise gently into the forever,
Carried by angels,
Where we'll be together again
In the presence of the Lord Almighty
For all eternity.

BETWEEN LOVERS

Before our enchanting acquaintance,
Our lives were full of dark devastation:
A road of constant forlornness
That absorbed our lives,
Swallowing us whole
Into the bowels of melancholia.
Loss of faith, and belief
In humanity, and God
We ran wild, we ran violently,
We dove blindly into the ways of the night,
Without care, without respect,
Without integrity, without remorse.
Self-annihilation—
We were imprisoned for too long,
Far, far too long,
Caged in the blackest of depression,
Embottled in the depths of drink,
No strangers to pain or disappointment;
Lies and broken promises were laid before our feet
Instead of the gifts of love.
Neglected and rejected by false lovers,
For years we hid in the shadows,
Camouflaging our true identities,
Sheltered away in the basement of reclusion,
Where our souls silently wept for love
To the rhythm of our aching hearts.

But all that insanity passed
On the day of our encounter,
That warm, beautiful, mystical day
When we fell in love with each other—
Madly, deeply in love—
Becoming lovers, and lovers we are,
Lovers to the utmost extreme.
Between lovers, as lovers do,
We opened the chamber doors to our hearts,
And a reservoir of love poured out of us,
Crystal clear and intoxicating.
We welcomed one another inside
With open arms, and tearful kisses;
Our souls embraced.
We solaced each other with purifying empathy
And with time and patience.
We healed one another's open wounds
With love, devotion, and surrender.
We gently polished away the blemishes of yesterday's miseries,
Reforming and restoring our deformed hearts
Back into their original state of beauty.

Between lovers—
It was time for us to love,
It was time to receive true love,
From one lover to another.
We shared our hearts in depth,
Allowing each other to explore freely
The inner recesses of our entities,
Blending our deepest thoughts,
Entwining our intimate secrets,
Collaging the passionate images of our psyches
Into a colorful picture of exotic, erotic love.
Our love—
Between lovers,
We made our own covenant of love:

Heart to heart, soul to soul,
That our passion will always remain incandescent,
Burning faithful, vigorous flames,
Full of vivacious, virtuous desires.
That our hearts were forever safe,
Sound, and secure;
That our love was precious
And as sacred as a holy temple.
Worshiping one another like an ancient religion
According to God's word,
We vowed to never allow anything to come between us,
Promised to keep everything in our love real
To cast away all illusions and doubts
From the mind, heart, and soul.
We swore to suffer on a bed of thorns
If we ever dreamt of sleeping with another individual.
Between lovers—
This is our oath of integrity.

The fires of admiration
Flared within our eyes.
Portals of purity,
Silent feelings said so much.
Between lovers
Within the apples of one another's eyes
We found our home
Me into you, you into me
No more loneliness, no more searching.
Lover, sweet lover,
We're no longer alone.
Between lovers—
Our piercing pupils of ignited intimacy
Melted our hearts of ice
Into pools of passion
Where we now swim freely
Within the fervent waters of our desires.

Between lovers—
Naked we swim
In our pool of tears
Washing each other with emotions
Bathing within the blood of our amorous hearts
That bleeds red tears of absolute love
Between lovers.

We love each other just as lovers do:
Without lines, or limits.
Unconditional love
Wrapped in the arms of fiery passion—
Lips to lips, soulful kisses,
Full of hunger and meaning;
Skin to skin, celestial caresses
Full of gentleness and excitement.
Locked together in love's tender embrace,
Eye to eye, boring into one another's soul,
Vised between hips,
All is bliss, all is bliss.
Between lovers, we are one.
Between lovers, one are we.
Between lovers, together forever.
Between lovers, our love eternally.
As lovers do
We hold our love ever so tight,
Just you and me forever
Letting our hearts sweetly flow
As lovers do.

Between lovers—
Kiss me with those sweet lips of wine,
Kiss my crying heart,
And tell me how deeply you're mine.
Between lovers—
Let me kiss you with my lips of fire.

Let me kiss your crying heart.
You're the only one that I desire.
Between lovers—
Hear the songs of our soul,
Listen to the whispers of our hearts.
This love we share is solid and complete.
From now on we'll never be lonely.
Between lovers—
Burning, burning, burning
Inside my heart.
Just for you:
Flames of undying love,
Yearning, yearning, yearning
Inside my soul.
Just for you.
You're the one I'm always thinking of.

Lover, sweet lover,
I love you—
Love you so much, it's excruciating.
I need you badly, badly I do,
That I constantly pine for your every touch.
Lover, sweet lover,
I can never have enough of you.
Between lovers—
Lover, lover, lover,
I love you,
And I love the way you love me too.
Between lovers—
Both day and night,
Believe me darling when I tell you
No one else will ever do.
Between lovers—
Lover, lover, lover,
I love you.

LOST WITHIN YOUR EYES

Through the windows of my soul,
I'm captured by the wonders of you.
Your lovely eyes take me away
To that special place of clarity
Where all things are beautiful.

Inside of you, there is a garden of beauty—
Ultimate beauty—
Countless rows of roses and grapes
Erotically entwined,
Oozing love in fragrance and taste.

The essence of you inebriates all my senses,
Filling my body and mind
With the sweetest high I have ever experienced.
The flavors of your passion are so deliciously rich
That I'm addicted to your nectar,
Constantly craving more.

Absorbed by your enchanted beauty
I'm lost within your eyes
But found by your love;
Embraced by your hunger,
I surrender my heart freely
For the passion that I have longed for
I have found within the depths of you.

ALWAYS WITH YOU

My heart, like the sun,
Blazes with passion;
Its fire consistently burns.
Though your seasons change,
I'm always with you.
In your times of grayness
And rainy days,
You may feel all alone,
Yet behind the black clouds
And all through the storm,
I'm always with you.

My soul, like the moon,
Glows with radiance;
Its light shines vigorously.
Though you're surrounded by darkness,
I'm always with you;
In your times of wandering
And seeking the wilderness,
You may lose your way,
Yet through all the gloom and eeriness,
My love for you will pierce the night.
I'm always with you.

ONLY YOU

Whenever I look into your eyes,
I see you, and only you—
Your soul a fire of pure intimacy
That blazes passion just for me.
Your beautiful heart embraces me
With welcoming arms of blissful love
And the sweetest lips I've ever tasted.
Your kisses are red as silky petals
Grown from the finest garden of roses.

Only you can bring me such comfort;
There is no love like your love,
No passion or desire as strong as yours,
That possesses me the way you do.
My heart belongs to you,
And only you do I faithfully cherish
With all of my innermost being.

Only you can please me, only you.
You fill my heart with overwhelming satisfaction.
Your love is the medication that heals my soul
When the world wounds me with its evil ways.
Your sweet love is the core of your beauty.
You repaired my broken life
And restored my aching heart back to health.

There are no riches on this earth greater than your love.
Your love is priceless, and incomparable.
Your gentle love eases my sorrows
And gives me the strength to live another day.
Because of your Christ-like nature,
I know the meaning of true love and affection.

Only you remembered me
When everyone else forgot;
When everyone else left me in the cold,
You took me into your heart.
Only you loved me enough to suffer
The same pains as I have;
You took my hand in yours
And have been with me ever since.

Only you are worthy of my heart
And all the love that's inside of me.
Only you do I love, adore, and treasure
Because you are who you are:
You are my one and only.
Only you do I love.
I love you, forever you,
Only you.

YOU PLUS ME EQUALS US

Our love is pure mathematics.
It's a very simple equation:
I love you, and you love me;
Therefore, we love each other.

To love each other, we must be together,
And to be together we must add each other's love.
You plus me equals us,
And in us is our love—
One solid love.

To subtract our love from each other
Would leave us separated:
Single, solo, alone.
Division would leave us in halves—
Half-hearted, half-loved.

But together as a whole,
Our love multiplies,
Becoming stronger and greater in unity.
You plus me equals us.
As long as we're together,
Forever us we'll be—
And that's good math.

FOR YOU

For you I give my every ounce of energy,
Devote myself to you completely
Without boundaries or conditions;
My love is exclusively yours.

I place my throbbing heart within your hands;
Feel its beat of passion, feel its desire,
Listen to its faithful rhythm play
An endless drum solo for you.

On a platter of solid affirmation,
I serve to you all of my deepest emotions,
Marinated in the nectar of my heart
And sautéed in the spices of my soul.
Taste the essence of my love,
For its recipe was written and prepared just for you.

Born to love you, and love you I do
With fervor and purity
Beyond all comprehension.
I was made for loving you,
To cherish, treasure, and adore
From the core of my existence,
To give you ultimate passion, and supreme felicity—
This is my fate—
For you.

WITHOUT YOU

Melancholy and solitude hold hands in the dark.
Like a candle without its flame,
It has no vitality.
Without you, I too have no energy.
I'm just an unlit stick of wax.

My love lies naked in the pit of my heart,
Seedy and shivering like an abandoned animal.
Your absence has lengthened immensely,
Leaving me lost within this vast forest
Where time is vague.

My life is empty whenever we're apart;
Like a tree without its leaves,
I'm winter bare,
Waiting, waiting for you,
Month after month,
As branches wait for spring.
Without you, I cannot bloom.

Without your love,
There is no life inside of me,
Only a cold dark void
That echoes throughout my body
Like a murmuring stream
That sounds like thunder in a valley of silence.

My heart, soul, and mind
Have no rhythm, balance, or clarity.
Everything is in slow motion and distorted.
And the hours between night and day
Seem so far away
Without you.

RAGING LOVE

Feeling of love—absolute love, raging love—
Possess my heart and soul.
You've knocked me to my knees
With such an overwhelming force of felicity
That I'm forever moonstruck.

Raging, raging, raging love
Boils my blood to the state of ecstasy.

Tidal waves of emotions arise,
Swelling my veins in a rush,
Flooding my body with passion and desire
Just for you,
Leaving me totally yours.

Raging, raging, raging love
Has blinded me with ardent romance.

Hurricane love
Furiously blows through my mind.
Thoughts of you all the time
Surround my consciousness,
Leaving me oblivious to this world.
You're all that my eyes see.

You're my life,
You and only you.
I love you.

Raging, raging, raging love
Has elevated my heart to celestial levels.

My love for you grows wildly,
Doubling in size with each passing day,
Beyond weights and measures,
Reaching astronomical heights,
Far into the realm of infinity.

ULTIMATELY BEAUTIFUL

I have never tasted nectar as delicious as yours;
Your lips are juicy as ripe peaches.
My tongue finds your kisses stimulating—
A refreshing drink
That leaves me in an enchanted state of loopiness.

You're beautiful, absolutely beautiful—
Everything about you is supreme.
Your qualities of being are so celestial
That every time I look into your eyes,
I see a realm of paradise.

Every time we touch, streams of light flow through my body
Their radiance erases the dark melancholy clouds
That cling to my lonely heart.
Enwrapped in the warmth of your luminous being,
You bathe me with your ebullient love.

Whenever we make love,
The union of our bodies is so intense
That our souls scintillate from the fusion of our passion,
Causing cascades of bliss to overflow our pulsating hearts,
Bring us into deeper levels of intimacy.

Absorbed into you completely,
I have never experienced such love.
You have taken me to new heights of ecstasy,
An atmosphere of intoxicating satisfaction,
Where all things are ultimately beautiful.

INAMORATO'S OATH

Prelude

(Late One Summer's Evening)

Hello my sweet inamorata.
I know it's very late,
And I'm deeply sorry if I woke you,
But you've been heavy on my mind
Every day my heart painfully pines to be with you.
Visions of your lovely face surround me wherever I go,
Inebriating my thoughts and reflexes with such force
That my whole being has become lovesick.

I desperately needed to see you tonight.
My soul is swollen with emotions just aching to be freed.
The lips of my heart have so much to share with you
That the throbbing is so unbearably loud;
It thunders throughout my consciousness like a wild tribal drum,
Keeping me sleepless for nights on end.

So come with me my little ladylove.
Let us out for a while.
The night is pleasant and the stars are wonderfully bright.
Let's go some place seclusive and tranquil
Where I may profess my deepest feelings for you.

The Profession

(Walking Hand in Hand on the Beach)

Sweetheart, I needed to be with you this evening
Because since we've been together,
My feelings for you have deepened immensely
And I no longer can suppress these overwhelming emotions within me.
I must express the depths of my love
Because I want you to know and understand
Exactly how much you truly mean to me.

Honey, you have become the center of my life,
The very core of my heart and soul,
To the point that I cannot bear being apart from you.
Whenever we're not together,
Each minute of the day drearily drags into hours.
As the second hand slowly tongues the face of time like dripping honey,
I need to share my life with you—
Just you and me, side by side,
Day after day till the years turn us gray,
Always and forever and a day,
I want to be with you.

Sweetheart, I'm deeply in love with you
And I'd like for you and me to merge into one state of completeness:
One heart, one soul, one love,
One us.

From my innermost recesses of existence,
Emotions of love escape from my heart
Like the essence of tropical flowers,
All combined into one intoxicating nectar,
An untamed mixture of exotic passion
That oozes just for you.

A deeper kind of love—
Real love, untainted love, unconditional love,
A love that knows no distance or restraints,
No shame or remorse,
A love that goes beyond all reason
Dives into the intimacy
Without fears or regrets,
A love that truly knows itself—
Every want, need, and desire
Expresses itself to its dearly beloved,
Giving itself entirely to its chosen one,
Freely, faithfully, forever.

From the vast abyss of my heart,
I profess my love to you;
An ocean of undying emotion
Flows through my body
With powerful waves of desire
That constantly rise for you.

My dear, sweet inamorata,
You are very precious to me;
My heart has eyes for you.
You, and only you do my eyes see.
Ever since our first encounter, I desired you,
Hungered for you, thirsted for you, loved you—
A crave so excruciating it brought tears to my eyes,
For I have never seen anyone more lovelier than you.
Your beauty has burned its image into my heart, soul, and mind forevermore.
You now dwell in every blood cell within my veins.
Your sweet name vibrates throughout my body,
Leaving me in a symphonic state of delirious love.

You're the goddess of my inner sanctuary,
Where my soul worships you religiously;
You're the empress of my inner realm,

Where my heart serves you absolute love;
You're the princess of my inner thoughts,
Where my mind meditates on you hour after hour.

You're the woman I've always dreamt of,
The lady I've always longed for,
And the love I want to spend the rest of my life with;
Lover, sweet lover, I love you.

The Oath

(Face to Face in a Loving Embrace)

From my heart to yours,
I vow my love to you.
Surrendering myself completely
To the tender mercies of your being,
I place my heart before your feet:
A gift of pulsating love for you.
I'm yours, infinitely yours.

I promise to cherish you perpetually,
Giving you every ounce of myself,
Communing with you always
In body, mind, heart, and soul
Showering you with unlimited love throughout the day.

I promise to serve you in every way imaginable.
Every part of my body belongs to you,
Aims to please your deepest needs, wants, and desires
Fulfill all your fantasies with extreme pleasure
Until your appetites have reached ultimate satisfaction.

I promise to be conscious of your feelings.
My mind will continuously think of you,

Focus on all your interests
And channel into your dreams and secrets,
Giving you my undivided attention
And nothing less.

I promise to dedicate the rhythms of my love to you.
My heart is a tambourine of serenades
That will play the sweetest melodies of passion,
Filling your everyday life with romantic harmony.

I promise to blaze the fires of my love into crevices of your being.
My soul is an inferno of rapture.
The inner mounting flame will consistently burn,
Keeping your heart toasty, tranquil, and ignited.

From this moment on, through kisses and tears,
I will devote my life to you,
Always serving you the nourishments of love,
Season after season.
Through all kinds of weather,
From celestial azure skies of summer
To the bitter black storms of winter,
I will provide my deepest affections,
Soothe you with endless delights.

Through life and death,
I will stand by your side,
Holding your hand safely in mine,
Keeping you close to my heart
Protecting you, comforting you, loving you,
Never ever letting you go.

From the rose gardens of heaven
Through the sulfury bowels of hell,
I will follow you.
No matter what path you choose in this life,

I will drift along that same road
And in the very end,
Whether we're rejoicing or suffering,
My soul will accept either of these two fates,
As long as I spend eternity with you.

I have never loved anyone as romantically as I love you,
And I will never love another as I love you now.
This love that I feel is a different love,
A foreign love, not of this atmosphere or era;
It's a love that comes once in a blue moon,
And not many are blessed to experience its profound beauty.
So, my lovely inamorata,
I vow all of my love to you:
This awesome, eccentric, ethereal love
That flows through me mystically,
Filling my heart and soul with ardent emotions
And uncontrollable fervor for you,
Only you, forever you.
I love you.

SATISFIED

I never believed that the cavity in my heart
Was ever capable of being repaired;
Its emptiness was of immeasurable depths,
A gouge of loneliness that constantly ached
Morning, noon, and night
Even in the faraway places of sleep,
My hunger for love was agonizing.

Then you flew into my heart
Like a bird to a tree;
The sweet passion of your songs
Embraced me with the warmth of your love
That filled my empty branches with life.
There are many beautiful things in this life,
And then there is you:
Wonderful, wonderful you,
Just you in a realm all of your own—
Splendid, extravagant, celestial.

Far more lovelier than anything else ever created
Because when the God almighty made you,
He made you exclusively for me
And He placed you in the center of my heart:
A human red rose.
A gift of absolute beauty,
Ultimate purity, and supreme love.

You're a sacred gem
From every angle of your brilliance.
I value your existence.
I'm fortunate to have you in my life,
Blessed to be loved by you,
And deeply grateful that you're mine.
You're a living jewel.

I hold you close to my soul
Where the fervor continuously rises
Into an inferno of true romance
That's incapable of ever being extinguished.

This fire that blazes inside of me
Burns just for you.
I love and adore you immensely.
I could never love another as profoundly as I love you,
For you are my one and only love,
Now and forevermore.
I'm satisfied.

FROM MY HEART TO YOURS

In the silence of night,
I close my eyes and breathe deeply.
Falling into a candlelight state of meditation,
I conjure up all my emotions for you
From the navel of my heart,
Drawing all my love to the lips of my soul.
Full of empyrean white passion,
I send you a fiery kiss
From my heart to yours.

On the blissful wings of consciousness,
My love soars freely through time and space,
Traveling on a current of divine energy.
Images of your beauty flood my mind
As my kisses fly across the evening sky
To where you lie sleeping in some distant dream.
My kisses lightly land on the fullness of your lips
Like a butterfly on an open petal.
You inhale me into the depths of your being,
Where I burst into a rainbow of tears,
Coloring your heart with the passions of my soul.

JUST YOU AND ME

Ever since we've been together,
There's no more lonely fire.
Our passions are no longer wasted in the arms of cold lovers,
Our hearts are no longer jaded,
And our souls are free from the whips of blue devils.
The love that we have for one another is genuine,
A love that's bound by nothing,
A love that knows no end.

Though the road has neither been straight
Nor smooth,
Our love has survived the curves of life,
And with each twist of the kaleidoscope,
We merged with each phase,
Never allowing the situation to ever separate our hearts,
No matter how devastating the storm.

We were born to love each other,
Destined to share our lives together.
From the time of our conception
The seed of love was planted,
And since then that seed began to grow within us,
Turning into a garden of wild passions
Beyond this world of synthetics
And into the empyrean
Where the erotic is freely expressed from the nooks of our hearts.

In an esoteric language,
Vows of eternity were whispered.
Sincere, sacred, and mystic,
Slowly undressing our inner selves,
We revealed our naked souls
Fell into the depths of love;
We were consumed by passion,
Burst into an ardent fire of oneness.

Through the divine eye,
We've entered a realm of sovereign beauty
Where our love has reached its zenith.
In the chambers of fervor,
We consummated our love,
Mixing, melting, marinating
Each and every desire of our hearts
Until the flavor was harmonized.
From a chalice of infinity,
We toast to our union,
Drink the wine of our love
Created just for you and me.

WAKE UP AND DREAM

Blow out the candle, my love,
And come lie beside me.
Lose yourself to the rhythmic songs of my heart
As I caress you to sleep.
Dream deeply within the comfort of my arms
And fall into the sweet state of euphoria,
Far away from this stressful world.

I, too, will follow you in slumber,
Down to the land of Morpheus
Where we'll awake in one another's embrace,
Naked, relaxed, and free.

Surrounded by exotic scents,
We inhale the essence into our souls.
Intoxicated by passion,
We explore the gardens of erotica
Row after row after row,
Devouring the fruits of ecstasy
Until our hunger has reached repletion.

After the feast of loving,
Extremely satisfied,
We drift off into a deep sleep
Only to wake up and dream once again
In the reality of one another's arms.

LIPS OF HONEY

The succulence of your orchid lips
Seep with erotic passion.
Through your deep soulful kisses,
I can taste the secret nectar of your heart,
And with each vibrant kiss,
Your lips fill my mouth with your sacred honey.
Pouring layers of amber sweetness down my throat,
You coat my wild heart with glazed solace,
Soothe my restless soul with your thick love.
Your loveliness has penetrated the center of my being,
Leaving me blissfully sedated
In a ambience of divine beauty
Where you smother me with omnifarious kisses,
Forever bathing me with your lips of honey.

LADY PETITE

You are the loveliest lady I've ever encountered.
Your petiteness floods a room with awesome aura,
Wonderful to behold, bella figure,
Your beauty is without mercy.
It's free, absolute, and untamed
And has overwhelmed my senses,
Drowning out the rest of the world.
I surrender all of my attention to you
And embrace the sovereignty of your existence with perfect clarity.

Though tiny in figure,
Your presence is astronomical in volume.
As a ladybug rests upon an incandescent flower,
Only your greatness is noticed.
Dominating the atmosphere with your loveliness,
Your fluorescence has transmitted its waves to my inner consciousness,
Peeling away the shades of gray with fervor,
Then biting deeply into the core of my soul,
Leaving your signature of love
Forever imprinted across my heart.

REKINDLED

After a great absence from one another's lives,
Fate has once again merged our paths,
Opening a new avenue of dreams for us to explore,
Heart to heart, soul to soul,
Beyond appearances into spiritual experience
Falling deeper into the realms of emotional intimacy
Where love, devotion, and surrender
Rest safely in the arms of infinity,
Untainted by vanity.

In the past, our love was silent and unripe,
Never reaching its full expression.
It was lost in youth and deeply missed.
Now found in maturity and great respect,
A fresh, red rose has been born,
A new candle has been lit,
A second chance has been rekindled.

Blessed by the joy of rediscovering you,
My long lost ladylove,
I warmly embrace you with all of my soul,
Welcoming you back into my life.
The gates to my heart are wide open for you.
Enter my innermost recesses of existence.
Allow me to bathe you with the nectar of my love.

Overwhelmed by bliss, I consume you into my heart and soul,
Savoring the reality of our reunion.
Through tears and kisses sweet emotions have arisen,
Both old and new,
Rekindling my heart into an inner mounting fire of endless passion.
What was once just a flame never fueled
Is now a blazing fire constantly fed—
A divine fire,
A fire of absolute unconditional love,
Burning freely, burning faithfully,
Burning just for you—
Eternally rekindled.

BELLA

Your eyes are full of vitality,
As powerful as the sun and moon
That both illuminate the celestial skies,
Blazing with fervor.
They reflect the higher realms of excellence with their awesome auras.
Just as their images mirror off the waves of the great oceans,
So it is with your alluring eyes
Which reveal your splendid being.

Season after season,
The warmth of your perfect love constantly blesses me.
By day, your ardent love nourishes my heart with profusive kisses.
No matter what kind of climate,
Your fiery love keeps my blood from ever getting cold.
By night, your enchanting love comforts my soul with divine caresses.
Nothing can ever obscure your radiance.
The power of your love keeps me romantically intoxicated.

You are a vision of sublime beauty;
I see your magnificent soul wherever I go.
Because I am in continuous union with you
In heart, soul, and mind,
Your lovely existence surrounds me always.
Through the secret conversations of the heart,
I have grown to know you, my beloved.

You, and only you, do I cherish.
You are my divine spouse whom I love and adore.
My heart desires no other.
I am religiously yours.

I alone love you, and my love for you is immeasurable.
No one else loves you as profoundly as I do.
Others love you for only the beauty they see for a season;
As the season comes to pass, so does their love.
But my love for you is timeless.
I love you for all seasons.
No external autumn can bring my love to pass
Because the beauty I see is within you:
A beauty that is ageless and evergreen.
I see in you what others do not see.
I see you with absolute clarity.
I love the unseen you, the real you.
I love you for yourself.
You are a garden of deep and endless passion,
A royal soil of extraordinary beauty.
Within you, there is no ugliness.
You walk in immaculate nakedness
Without vulgarity, shame, or vanity.
You are made in God's image.
There is nothing to add, subtract, or change.
You are a perfection of loveliness
Made from Heaven's hands.
You are ultimately beautiful.
You are forever the love of my life.

FEAR NOT LOVE

Fear not love.
For love is not your enemy.
Rejection is the fearful foe that cripples the heart of vitality.
The absence of love is the death of the soul.
True love never seeks to injure;
Its only desire is to serve.
Fear not love, for love fears not you.
Listen to the whispers of your heart.
Examine your feelings with discernment.
Know and understand the truth of love's purpose.
Be stagnant no more.
Follow your heart, follow your heart.

Don't be afraid to give love another chance.
Rebuild your broken dreams by forgiving the past.
Let not the debris of yesterday's promises obstruct your life.
Put your uncertainties to rest.
Believe in love once again.
Allow me to love you here and now.

I understand how you're feeling
Because I've been there myself before:
Lied to by selfish hearted souls
Who knew neither love nor integrity.
Don't let their poisonous tongues infect your heart.

For a heart that's afraid to love is a love denied,
And a love denied is a life of fear.
True love knows no fear.
Therefore, open your heart and love again.
Love freely, love fearlessly.
Love, and be loved,
For the essence of life is love,
And a life without love is dratted.

So come, take my hand and fear not love.
My heart is genuine.
Believe in love, as I believe in love.
Let love take its course.
Release your heart from its dungeon of darkness
And embrace the light of love,
A perfect love, an eternal love,
A love that casts out all fear.

HUSBAND AND WIFE

(A Marital Oath)

From this day forward,
Your life will no longer be alone.
I place this ring upon your finger
And vow my life to you
With all my heart, soul, and mind.
I freely give myself to you in holy matrimony
In love, devotion, and trust,
As God is my witness.

I promise to never wander from your side.
This world of vanity has nothing that I desire.
Inside your heart, I have found my refuge,
Where true love blazes with purity.
I will walk with you through life's journey,
Heart to heart, soul to soul,
One flesh in unison,
Without fear or doubt.
And if calamity comes our way,
We'll stand together in faith,
For hope, grace, and mercy will see us through.

Through triumphs, thrashes, or ties, I will remain steadfast.
Whether in poverty, security, or wealth,

I will protect, support, and serve you.
Through weeping, rejoicing, infliction, or euphoria,
I will envelop you with care, kindness, and prayer.
And if the Devil thrusts his trident,
I will beat him down with the Sword of the Spirit,
Because no matter how dire the consequences,
I will never leave or forsake you.
I'm forever yours, forever yours.

I promise to respect and appreciate the loveliness of your persona
And to fulfill it constantly with joy and pleasure,
Acknowledging the beauty of all your qualities
Those are the gifts of heaven.
I promise to love and honor you endlessly
From the very core of my soul.
I pledge this oath of marriage in sacred agreement,
In accordance with God's Holy Word,
Till death do us part.

A DEEP BLUE FIRE

From the first time I saw your pretty face,
Starbursts of sapphire lights appeared before my eyes.
Your beauty touched me so profoundly that I was overwhelmed by fever.
Love ignited my soul, swelling my heart with sweet desire,
Sending a burning sensation throughout my body
Like some secret love potion.

After tasting the essence of your lips,
I've become a true believer,
That when love strikes the heart,
It's impossible to deny its existence.
I'm forever moonstruck by this blissful revelation
That flows freely through my veins like lava.
My heart's on fire, a deep blue fire, for you.

This inner mounting passion has reached a wild roar.
No longer bound by uncertainty,
On the wings of love I fly.
Without fear, my heart is open.
I want to share my life with you
Because that's what true love is all about,
From one heart to another.

Within the chambers of my heart,
There's this deep blue fire,
Burning with fervor and mystery.
These flames of love burn just for you,
As bright as the moon, endless as the stars.
My hunger for you is astronomical.
Enter into this loving realm and make yourself comfortable.
Feel the warmth of my blazing lips kiss your entire being.
Allow the flames to envelop you.
Become one with me in this deep blue fire.

This deep blue fire lives and breathes to enrapture you
In heart, soul, and mind,
To serve, treasure, and protect you,
To be faithfully yours for all eternity.
I need you, I want you, I love you.
Be forever my soulmate,
Because a love this sacred must be from the divine will of God.

A WOMAN LIKE YOU

A woman like you is rare,
Cut from the ancient cloth of integrity
That was woven by the Word of God
Back when reverence was practiced with fervor instead of duty.

A woman like you, who's virtuous and serene,
Shines brightly as the heavens,
And is a crown of blessings to her husband,
Worth far more than any earthly treasures.
Your heart is a gift of celestial love,
Free from vanity.

A woman like you loves, trusts, and fears the Lord above all things.
This pure devotion reveals your true identity:
An imitation of Christ
That pours from your soul with such passion, grace, and fire,
I'm overwhelmed with bliss.
This is who you are:
Beautiful in all your ways,
My darling, my wife,
Forever my queen.

SMILE

Smile.
Smile for me
If not for anyone else.
Just smile for me.
Smile, my dear lady,
Because there is no smile on this earth
More wonderful than yours.

Smile.
Smile for me
Not only with your tender lips
But with your lovely eyes,
For they are dovelike and gentle
And full of overwhelming brilliance.

Smile.
Smile for me.
Only your smile fills my heart with joy.
And every time you do
It makes me smile too.
And when I do smile,
I smile just for you.

ALL I TRULY NEED

I think that you're very lovely,
And every time I look into your beautiful mystic eyes,
My heart swells with love
And a fervent fire that has no end.
Your pretty face always comforts me.
Leaving me in a daze of blissful starlight emotions
Which only you can cause,
You, my love, my darling,
It is the dream I've been waiting for.
And now that you're mine
I will never let you go.
I will love you always, forever and a day,
Giving you the best of love
From the deepest recesses of my heart and soul.
You're the only woman on this planet for me
Because your love is the key note that gives my heart its rhythm.
Without you, there's no harmony in my life.
You have filled my life with music, song, and dance.
For this I'm immensely blessed
And have no desire for another.
You're all I truly need.

WILL YOU EVER REALIZE?

Will you ever realize the storm is over,
That the tornado has long passed away,
And that the sun is shining, and the birds are singing?
Though not forgotten, yesterday is gone, forever gone,
And all those horrible, selfish, stupid men
Who have lied, cheated, and humiliated you are gone as well.
So why, why, why are you still rummaging through the debris,
Weeping over broken promises made by fools,
Who are not worthy of your tears?

One's life was not designed to be lived alone
But to be shared with another,
In unison of heart, soul, and mind,
Crowned in one flesh in holy matrimony,
To have and to hold dearly,
To love and to cherish exclusively,
Never leaving one another's side until death calls.
This is my belief, my faith, my religion,
Which I could give to you if you allow me.
Will you ever realize how deeply I love you?

A VINEYARD OF FERVOR

I have always believed in the essence of love,
That its vitality is absolute, empyrean, and everlasting,
And that everyone possesses a hidden vineyard deep within their hearts,
A secret place of sharing the core of oneself,
Where all is bliss and all is free,
Where the self is able to unleash its passion without fear of judgment,
Revealing its beauty that's both unconditional and deathless,
A celestial realm where true lovers meet at the table of erotic grapes
To drink the wine of their desires,
Becoming inebriated on the fruit of their emotions,
Falling insanely in love,
Forever to rejoice within the arms of one another's souls.
After opening the gates of their inner gardens,
They welcome one another with soulful kisses
As they explore the countless rows of their love.
Once in its depths,
They mix the seeds of passion into the soil of their hearts,
Showering each other with untainted, crystalline love.
Together they bloom in a lover's embrace,
Entwined into one vine—
A spiritual vine—
That can never be separated,
Not in this lifetime
Nor the hereafter.

For quite sometime,
A stirring of powerful emotions have been breathing deep within my soul,
An endless love pulsating within my veins,
Brewing love, fermenting love, pure love,
A passion sighing throughout the passages of my heart,
Echoing love in search of love,
Yearning to love and be loved,
By my destined lover.

When you came into my life,
I knew that ultimate love was found.
Your eyes bore the fruit of divine love—
A love supreme that I have painfully pined for for years.
Joined at the entrance of our gardens, we unlocked the gates
Allowing the vines of our hearts to be sacredly love-knotted.
Blending our seeds of love, we roped into wholeness,
Forever unbreakable, just you and me,
A vineyard of fervor.
For years, you were an enigma,
A secret love within the aisles of my heart.
Glimpses of your beauty flowed through my mind
While your identity remained obscured.
Revealment came with time and taste.
Over the years, I became a connoisseur of kisses,
Possessing the ability to differentiate character,
Sampling the emotions of hearts,
Until you came along and kissed my soul with your fervent lips,
Intoxicating me with your absolute love.

I have traveled through valleys of vineyards
In search of a fervent wine:
One perfect heart of flavor
That would constantly be filled with divine passion.
I have tasted all kinds of grapes—
Some bitter, some sweet, some fine—
Taking the time to savor,

But none of them captured my heart, soul, and mind
Like the way your ebullient lips have.
Your kisses are ardently superior.

After tasting the flavor of your love,
I have become completely drunk on you.
Only your kisses do I thirst for.
No one else's lips compare to yours.
Your love is a highly potent beverage,
A sweet remedy for any disease.
Ever since I drank your wine, my heart's been on fire.
From the moment I tasted the sincerity of your kisses,
I knew that the essence of your heart was not diluted.
The pulp of your lips was just for me,
Our mouths matched perfectly
As our tongues danced soul to soul
To the sacred music of our hearts.

Two hearts inflamed,
Our hearts wildly kissing fire to fire,
Merging into one fire,
Our fire,
An undying fire.
Blazing love, incandescent love, our love
Licking, lapping, loving,
Purifying every crevice of our innermost beings,
Bringing sweet peace to our restless lives.
Through heated soul kissing, naked emotions were expressed,
Freeing our passions that have been preserved for years.
Together our hearts cried tears of joy.
Drunk with fervor and fruition,
We celebrated the marriage of our souls,
No longer alone or lonely.
Our love has become one.

Your breath a fresh bottle of opened wine
Pours out sweet love for me,
Solacing me with the most vivacious kisses I have ever experienced.
Your heart is truly a vineyard of intense love
Where the grapes of eternal passions grow,
Your soul a wine cellar of bliss
Where I may indulge in the fiery spirits of your love
And drink until my heart's content.
The heat of your love flows deeply into my blood with each delightful kiss,
Each one more stimulating and juicier than the last.
The divinity of your love fills my body with overwhelming warmth and
tranquility,
Leaving my skin aglow.
I crave greatly for the succulence of your lips,
To taste the ripeness of only your kisses,
To devour the grapes of your heart,
To forever lose myself within the state of enchanted madness,
For there is no drink upon this earth
More deliciously intoxicating than the wine of your lips.

I have tasted the lips of many
And all they had to offer was watered-down love.
Their love was without depth, fire, or emotion.
Their kisses always left my soul feeling empty, cold, and lonely.
True love is spiritual within a realm all of its own,
Its value is beyond appraisal,
And nothing of this world can ever compare to it.
There is nothing of this world that I desire,
For its possessions will pass away with time,
But the vineyard within your heart
Will continue to bear the fruit of your love.
Now and forevermore, I surrender my heart to you.
Your love is worthy of endless devotion.
You have become my religion,

Because through your kisses
I have found supreme love.
Inside the sanctuary of your heart,
I have obtained freedom,
And with the union of our souls,
I have embraced infinity.

PRECIOUS

There are many things in this world of great value,
But none of them compare to you.
Nothing possesses the equality of beauty
That you so wonderfully display.
Your elegance is of a celestial nature,
Far more precious than earthly riches.
Designed by God's hands,
Your value is beyond all measures.

Your eyes are the windows of paradise,
A realm where all is bliss.
I've wandered through your garden of spices
Where the savory scents enveloped me.
The recipes of your heart are superb—
The finest cuisine of love I ever tasted.
There is no other dish for me.
I'm awed by your beauty.
I surrender, I surrender.

I have no regrets, none at all,
For submitting my heart to you.
You're a very special lady,
Genuine through and through,
Precious, sacred, and absolute.
You're a heavenly dream;
Falling in love with you came easy,
For you're the loveliest creature I've ever encountered.

I LOVE YOU

Amorous tears fall like rain;
Each drop whispers your sweet name
As it flows into hidden streams
Where I hold you dearly in my dreams.
In the depths of my mind,
You're with me all the time.
Passions for you blaze out of control
Because the fires of love possess my soul.

I love you, I love you, I love you—
O how deeply I do, faithfully love you
Love you … love you … love you.

These words of love can never really express the way I love you,
Nor can my actions ever be so profound
Because the music of my heart
Is a love composed of a greater sound.

My heart strums a million guitars,
Playing my emotions beyond the stars,
Into a galaxy far from here,
Where my love dominates the atmosphere;
A love serenade written just for you
With lyrics that express a deeper view
Of all the feelings that I hold inside
Within my soul where only you abide.

Look into my eyes and see the fire
Its flame burns not of normal traditions
Feel the passion of its raw truth
Because my love for you is beyond all religions.

I love you ... I love you ... I love you
O how deeply I do, faithfully love you
Love you ... love you ... love you.
I love you.

MAGNETIC EMOTIONS

I saw you standing there,
A red rose full of flare.
My heart filled with such intrigue
That your beauty took me to a deeper league.

Into the warmth of your eyes I'm drawn,
Like a bee to the sweetness of flowers;
Lured by some unseen force,
I'm captured by your mystic powers.
Magnetic emotions pull me deeper into you
Where our true identities meet face to face;
Our souls kiss the kiss of love
As our hearts romantically embrace.

Lovely, lovely you:
I've never seen such a splendid view;
Hypnotized by surprise,
Your lusty eyes got my blood to rise.

You're beautiful, elegant, and divine;
I'm bound by your loveliness like an anchor to a ship;
Awestruck by your celestial kisses,
My heart bursts into ardent flames.
Into intimate depths I dive

Submerged in immeasurable passions
Attracted to your heart, I cling to you
And absorb the love you're bleeding.

Words cannot express
How my heart you so easily undressed;
Naked I now stand,
Totally yours in the palm of your hand.

I followed the path of my emotions
Which lead me to your love source.
Locked to you forever and ever
By love's invincible force,
Magnetic emotions have fused us together.
From just one spark
Heart to heart, soul to soul,
True love has made its mark.

SOLACE

Don't cry my love, don't cry.
Everything will be just fine.
No matter how grey the sky,
All good things come with time,
So don't you cry.

I know you've been through some bad moods,
Suffering from those damn flashes,
Constantly changing from red to blue.
Just remember Phoenix rose from its ashes,
And so will you ... so will you.

Come to me, my darling.
Let me wipe the tears from your pretty face.
Don't be frightened, my little starling.
Come nest yourself in my embrace.
I hold you so dear, so don't you fear.
My heart is a safe place.
I'll help you through this despair
With love, support, and solace.

Calm down, breathe deep.
Don't allow yourself to seethe.
Put your anger to sleep.
Don't drown; slowly breathe.
Take small steps; don't leap.

Take your time; don't you hurry.
Just live life for today.
Don't fill your heart with so much worry.
There's always another way
To overcome the fear and flurry.

Let yourself be absorbed;
Feel my fervor and grace.
Know that you're adored
Beyond all time and space.
So don't you cry my love, cry no more.
Just take life at your own pace
Don't be afraid to unlock the door
Because you'll always have my love, support, and solace.

THE GIFT

Taken from God's treasure chest
And placed into my desolate life,
The greatest gift I've received
Is you, my precious wife.
There is no other woman who compares to you.
You're truly divine.
I've been extremely blessed
Since our hearts have been entwined.

Your love for me knows no distance;
It's as blue as the endless sky.
Into the stars you have taken me,
Where our naked souls freely fly.
Soaring on current of raw emotion,
You embrace me with wings of fire.
Losing myself within your love,
I surrender to sweet desire.

You're the jewel of my heart,
The one I've always longed for,
A diamond of radiant being
That has ignited my life forevermore.
No more mines to search,
No more waters to drift—
You're all I'll ever want or need
Because your love is the ultimate gift.

AFTER ALL THIS TIME

After all this time,
Our love still beats a steady pace.
Through all the fears and tears,
Our hearts remained face to face,
Kissing … caressing … loving.

After all this time,
Our souls are still yearning.
The fervor has never ceased,
Both day and night, the candles are burning—
Passion … desire … romance.

Time has not weakened the fire
Nor has distance diluted the flame.
Bound by the jaws of integrity,
This marriage is an eternal reign.
Heart-shaped links of unity
Grow with each new day.
Time and distance could never break this marriage,
Nor can it ever steal our love away.

After all this time,
Our hearts are still adoring.
From the secret passages of our souls,
The rapture is still roaring—
Love … devotion … surrender.

After all this time,
Our marriage has remained sublime.
Through sickness, health, for better or worse,
I'm still yours, and you're still mine—
Willing ... wanting ... waiting.

THE PICTURE

All I have is this picture of you,
Which keeps my heart alive and yearning.
I stare into the apples of your eyes
And see passion's fire faithfully burning.
I feel the warmth of your loving smile,
Its depth as great as the infinite sky.
I lose myself in the dreams of tomorrow
That await for both you and I.

This picture of you sings secret songs,
Songs of intimate emotion,
Sung in a tone that only my heart could hear,
With words of unconditional devotion.
I could hear the music of your soul
Softly playing from within your eyes,
A love serenade composed
In the sweetest melody of sighs.

This picture always comforts me
When I'm down and ready to fold.
It brings me closer to your heart
When the nights are lonely and cold.
Your beauty is always with me
Because your love is captured in time.
The intensity of your loving stare
Is forever engraved in my heart, soul, and mind.

DREAMS OF YOU

Visions of you storm my mind:
I see us together in another place and time,
Walking by the ocean hand in hard,
Just laying naked in the sand,
Making love to the rhythm of the sea—
We are one in perfect harmony.
You come to me in the silence of night,
Possessing all of my body with your beautiful sight,
With red roses blooming from your hair
And pure love pouring from your stare.
You kiss my lips with fervent desire,
Setting my heart and soul on fire.
Dreams of you are a blissful pretense
That always simulates my inner sense,
Leaving my soul in absolute awe.
You're the only one my heart weeps for.
Everything is a perfect view,
When I'm lost in these sweet reveries of you,
And I don't care if I never awake,
Because this kind of freedom no one can ever take.

Into a secret forest we wander
Where on our love we ponder.
Like the wings of a dove,
We elevate a love

To the state of divinity—
Our love is written into infinity.
In a room full of candlelight,
Our naked bodies dance in flight.
Wine and roses scent the air,
Intoxicating the atmosphere.
Our love can never come undone
Because our hearts and souls are forever one.
Dreams of you keep you close to me;
In my heart you'll forever be.
Even though we're apart,
Distance will never conquer my heart.
My love for you will always survive
Because my dreams keep you alive.
So close your eyes and dream of me too,
And feel the passion I feel for you.

GARDEN OF LOVE

Into the depths of you I have fallen,
Losing myself in absolute bliss,
Aisles and aisles of endless fervor;
Never have I known a love like this.
Beauty, such beauty, your beauty,
Has devoured me whole.
Awed by your enchanted eyes,
Your loveliness has possessed my soul.

From the first taste of your delicious grapes,
I became intoxicated with love.
Ever since that mystical awakening,
You're all I'm ever thinking of.
Your ruby red roses stimulate my senses—
A fragrant love potion
Captured by the wonders of you.
My heart soars on wings of emotion.

Every row of your garden is heavenly,
Each path tranquil and hypnotic.
Deeper and deeper in love I fall
For your beauty is so exotic.
Your grapes are saturated with love,
And your roses a fiery red splendor;
Your garden is a realm of addictive delights
Where into your soil, my seed I surrender.

CHIMES OF THE HEART

The sound of chimes is ringing;
The compositions of my heart,
Harmonized emotions gently scale
As my soul plays the sweetest love songs for you.
The bells of fervor flare with intimacy
As the percussions soar across the heavens.
There is no greater expression of love
Than through the intercourse of instrumental vibes.
Words can never capture the orgasmic beauty I feel when I'm with you.

DISTANCE

We've been together a very long time,
Long enough to know when something is wrong.
It's not good to keep things bottled up,
So confide in me. Hold nothing back.
Speak your mind. Express your heart.
Don't let this distance go beyond our horizon.
Though at this time I'm unable to be by your side,
I'm with you always in spirit.
Just close your eyes and dream of me.
You'll see both day and night.
Open your heart to me with ink—
I'm just a pen and paper away.
So hold on tightly and don't give up.
Our love is too strong to allow distance to break us.
God will see us through this difficulty.
Have faith, trust and hope.
So don't you fret, my darling.
I'll be home soon.
I love you.

UNISON

Our love faithfully flows uninterrupted
As we walk together in concord,
Heart to heart, soul to soul.
Passion, grace, and peace have found their home.
No more loneliness, no more hunger—
You're everything I've ever imaged you'd be.
I'm satisfied, and deeply, deeply blessed.
I pine for no other.
You're truly my ladylove.

Compatible in our ways, one harmonious mind;
Our hearts pulsate in perfect synchronicity.
As our emotions run through our veins like wildfire,
There is no other love greater than this.
When two hearts burst into one fervent blaze,
Fused into a sculpture of romantic art,
Erotically entwined beauty,
And with each new day our fire grows beyond
Into the vast abyss of space
Where our souls are forever engraved in the heavenly stars.

WE AS ONE

You have filled my life with fervent bliss
All from one amatory kiss.
You cleaned me up when I was a mess,
With patience, love, and tenderness.
By setting new foundations down,
You changed my whole life around.
Now I'm a brand new man
Because you took the time to understand
That I was still caught in yesterday's storm
So you gave me your love and kept me warm.
When I realized what you were really about,
My frozen heart began to thaw out,
And as my feelings began to grow,
Both you and I began to flow.
In unison our love excelled
Into a relationship forever compelled
To love, honor, and respect
No matter how we may reflect.
To never judge or condemn when one offends,
Only forgive and make amends,
Always remaining together
Through all kinds of weather,
Merging our passion and desire
Into one amorous fire.
Blazing like the heavenly sun,
Together forever we as one.

AFTER YOU

If you were to leave me tomorrow
In the dead of night unseen
While I lay soundly sleeping
Lost in the grips of some far away dream,
I would forgive you.

And if you were to ever stop loving me
For whatever reason,
My heart would remain the same.
Even though yours has changed season,
I would still love you passionately within my heart.

There is only one you,
And you're my one and only.
No one could ever replace you;
After you, I'd be lost and lonely.
No one would ever take the time to love me
Like the way you have through the years.
No one could capture the essence you possess;
After you, my life would be in tears.

After you there'd be no more sunrises;
Into the darkness I would wander,
Disappearing into the night,
Where my life would slowly be squandered
Over losing you.

Though the flame may be gone,
The candle will always remain,
Never being lit by another
For its wick length will forever stay the same
After you.

DELICIOUS

Behind your dark lovely eyes,
Candles of passion dance ever so sweetly.
The pulp of your heart drips with juicy love
That has drenched my arid life with pleasure.
Deep and soulful,
Your succulent lips have been spiritual nourishment,
Savoring my bitter heart
With kisses addictively delicious.

Every kiss from your mouth is distinctive
And as tasty as a bowl of exotic fruit.
Drunk with fervor,
I'm drawn deeper into your orchards.
Safe within your garden,
You embrace me with erotic delights.
Full of appetizing flavor,
You have elevated my soul to ecstatic levels.

You have served me the finest dishes of passion,
Intimately prepared only for a lover,
And with each serving you've given healthy shares—
Each plate more delicious than the last.
You're a master chef of lovemaking,
And your specialties will never go bland,
Because your heart is an exquisite restaurant
And you're the sultriest meal I've ever tasted.

FEELINGS OF LOVE

My feelings for you are immense—
Always have been, forever will be.
From the first day we met,
I knew you were the one for me.
Ever since our first kiss,
You've been my only lover,
And now that we're together,
I'll never need another.

I'm satisfied with your kisses
And unique loving touch.
My heart desires only you—
I love, love you so very much.
Believe me when I tell you
You're forever on my mind.
Deep inside my being,
You're with me all the time.

Listen to the whispers of my soul,
Understand these feelings I proclaim;
Know the love of my heart
As well as you know your name.
Feel my love embrace you
As I kiss your spiritual sores,
And always remember, now and forever,
That my heart is faithfully yours.

ELYSIAN CLIMAX

Into the astral skies we soar,
Our hearts locked in a lovemaking embrace,
Entwined together forevermore
On the passionate wings of celestial space.
Flying freely across the mystic night,
Our desires explore into forbidden zones;
Ascending into erotic flight,
Our souls release ecstatic moans.

Me into you and you into me,
Our spirits connected from every shore;
Sexual expression artistically free,
Our love creating a distinctive roar.
Riding the currents from all directions,
Copulation has reached eccentric delights.
We've excelled to the state of Elysian heights.

US

Who would have ever thought
That two lost souls would discover
Solace, solidity, and soundness
The way we have in each other.
Dreams of love have become a reality;
Our ship of desires has finally arrived.
No more illusions of romance;
Our hearts will no longer be deprived.
In perfect harmony,
Our souls sing love's symphony,
Expressing emotions for one another
In a soft serenade of empathy.
Yesterday's broken hearts are long gone;
In each other we have found trust.
No longer alone, our love has found its home
Because we have become us.

FEELING YOU

Your presence possesses the center of my heart,
And all through my blood stream you flow,
Pumping your sweetness into my life—
You're with me wherever I go.
From roosters to crickets,
You're constantly on my mind.
Embedded deep within my soul,
Your love surrounds me all the time.

From Aphrodite to Venus
And all other goddesses in between,
Smitten by your beauty
You're the perfect dream.
Because all that is, you are—
From the seeds of existence, to the highest celestial view,
Embraced by your divine nature,
I'm forever feeling you.

LOST WITHOUT YOU

Coldness surrounds me like an arctic landscape
Whenever we're apart,
And darkness covers me like a black cape
When you're not close to my heart.
Loneliness is a cancer
That eats at my soul;
When we're not together my life's a disaster,
Chaotic, and out of control.
My loneliness is so immense.
I'm lost without you, so very lost without you,
That nothing makes any sense.
It's like the sky without its blue—
Everything becomes gray and dense.

My world has no meaning
When I'm all alone.
It's like sleeping without dreaming,
Or living in a house where nobody's ever home.
Without you, my heart is bare.
My life is full of empty spaces.
It's like aimlessly walking nowhere,
Wearing shoes without their laces.
I'm lost without you, so very lost without you.
It's like sitting at a table of seven,
Or a crime without a clue;
It's like having a hell without a heaven.
Darling, sweet darling, I'm lost without you.

SHE

She made a believer out of me
By giving me her love exclusively;
She melted my heart with just one kiss
And proved to me true love exists.
She has her own unique style;
She can comfort me with just a smile.
Her loving qualities are of an ancient breed;
She's the only woman I'll ever need.
She rescued me from a sea of desperation
And entered my realm of alienation.
No longer lonely or alone,
We now share a world of our own.
She pulled me out from the mire
And turned my cold heart into fire.
With each kiss, my flames grew higher;
Now she's all that I desire.
She casted away my eclipse
With candle flame kisses from her lips,
Then she wiped the tears from my eyes
And gave to me clear blue skies.
She took my broken heart and made it whole
The moment she embraced my sighing soul.
Her loving beauty has changed my life
Ever since the day she became my wife—
And what a wonderful wife she has been,

With a heart of roses and a soul of satin.
She has given me more than I've ever dreamed of.
She's a woman of empyreal love.
She's the one who set my bonded soul free
Because she took the time to really know me.
By loving me passionately
We became one, forever one are we.

ROSE OF MY HEART

A rose through my heart
Like an arrow of love,
Shot from Cupid's bow.
You were sent from above.
With love as sharp as a knife,
Your beauty cut me so deeply
That I made you my wife.
Beautiful, beautiful you,
Warm as the sun,
You planted yourself inside my heart,
Together now we grow as one.
You bloom all through my body
Like wild roses do;
Your essence intoxicates me—
I surrender my love to you.
Your lips are soft as petals:
Red, silky, and sweet;
Your kisses are the nectar of my soul
That make my life complete.
You're the reason for my joy and happiness;
Your love fills all of my needs.
You're my vivid vivacious red rose
In this wicked world of weeds.

ALIVE

There were many times in the past
I was unable to smile,
But you always seem to comfort me
With your sweet gentle style.
You filled my heart with understanding
And eased my mind with a touch;
Whenever I looked into your eyes,
I always saw so much.

There is a fire within my heart
Blazing out of control;
Flames of passion burn for you
From the depths of my soul.
And when we're alone together,
Our feelings flow free.
With a hug, a kiss, and a whisper,
It's forever you and me.

With you in my life,
I know I will survive.
No matter how dark the world may get,
I'll always feel alive.
You're my heavenly treasure,
The ruby of my life;
You'll always remain precious to me,
My darling, my love, my wife.

BURNING HEART

You're the one for my heart that bleeds;
You give my heart everything it needs.
You're the sweet flame that feeds the fire,
Warming my soul with uncontrollable desire.
A flaming heart that burns for you,
It cries at night flames of blue.
A special love burning inside of me,
A burning heart for your eyes to see.
You were the spark from the very start;
Your name is burned across my heart.
The flames for you get higher and higher;
I love you, I love you, my heart's on fire.
Pulsation is strong, my mind a daze;
This love for you an eternal blaze.
So have no fear, have no doubt:
This flame of mine will never burn out.

WORDS CAN NEVER SAY

Words can never say
What you truly mean to me,
Because my feelings are beyond
What words can ever be.
Love is not just a four-letter word;
Its essence is more than it seems.
No dictionary can ever define
What true love really means.

Loving you is an emotion
Which no words can ever find;
Love for you comes from my heart
And not from my mind.
Love is an invisible existence;
It's felt by those who really know.
That love is far much more
Than words and actions can ever show.

I could never say in words
What words just can't explain,
Like the torment of missing you
Is beyond the definition of pain.
Or what it's like to kiss your lips
And have you sleep close to me,
Or what it's like to touch your face
And caress you ever so tenderly.

No words can ever describe
That type of human emotion;
Words are as far from me
As the heavens are from the ocean.
And words can never capture
The depth of my heart faithfully true,
Or even understand the meaning why
I'm so madly in love with you.

Love is a force of passion;
This fervor arises from those who are absolutely real.
It's something powerfully precious
That only the heart and soul can feel.
Because in all our human wisdom
We'll never find a way
To truly express our emotions
With words that can never say.

WEDDING BAND

This ring is sacred, absolute and true;
It holds the vows made between us,
Binding our hearts together,
Making us of one flesh, and of one mind.
This ring costs less than an engagement ring;
Once bought, it can't be sold.
But its spiritual value is greater than all the diamonds of this world,
For this ring is holy, and blessed by the Lord Almighty.
It's the bond of our faith, and the unity of our souls;
This ring is assurance of our love, honor, and devotion
To serve and protect one another faithfully
From all calamity, assaults, and temptations of the Devil,
For this ring is eternal.
It holds our trust and belief in God and His Word;
He alone has joined us together in holy matrimony
And that no man dare to ever separate.

GROWING IN LOVE

O love, please forgive me
For my lack of abilities,
Like not saying the things I should
Because of my silly insecurities.
I know I don't always speak my heart,
But that doesn't mean I don't love you.
I'm just so lost within your love
That I don't know what to say or do.
I know you understand how I'm feeling;
You do these things so many times yourself,
Like keeping your emotions within your heart
Hidden on some distant shelf.
But once we expose our feelings in the light
And release all our built-up tears.
Expressing our love freely to one another
Is how we'll conquer our fears.

Nobody ever said love was easy
Or even that there was no pain,
But true love will stand and fight
Because there's so much in love to gain.
This is all part of growing in love
And together we'll make it through;
I'd rather go through the pains of love
Than the rest of my life without you.

I know the loneliness that you suffer
All alone in your bed at night,
Shedding your tears into the pillow
Wishing I was there in your arms so tight.
O love, how I know these feelings;
I too suffer this lonely hell,
Lying awake in hunger for you
With the fear of losing you as well.

When in love, patience is a must;
Growing into each other takes time,
To understand the emotions of our hearts
And the thoughts within our minds.
Growing in love is to listen and learn,
Taking the time to really know,
Giving ourselves faithfully to one another
And letting our innermost feelings show.

I know sometimes I get down and weary
And my feelings become hard to explain;
I get so deep within myself
That I feel as if I'm going insane.
I try to open my heart to you,
But sometimes it's under lock and key.
I want so desperately to give myself over—
O love, come set my bonded soul free.

Let's grow together in love
And become wiser as the days go on,
Accepting the bad as well as the good,
Because every rose possesses a thorn.
Let's not allow any thorns to come between us
Or cut us and make us bleed;
We must stay strong, forgive our wrongs,
And give each other the love we need.
Growing in love is to confess our feelings,

So I'm confessing my love for you;
I need you, need you forever in my life,
Because no one else will ever do.
I love you, O how I love you;
My desire just tears me apart.
O love, you belong inside of me,
Deep within my aching heart.

We've been together for a while now
And we've come such a long, long way;
It's time we let go of the past
And forgive the sins of yesterday.
It's you and me against the world,
All its problems and strife;
Let's hold on together, never surrender—
Our love will see us through this life.
Forgive me for the times I've hurt you
And caused your pretty heart to cry;
I never meant to say the things I said
That day when I said good-bye.
I would never hurt you intentionally.
I'm just not that kind of guy.
So forgive me for all those times
We didn't see eye to eye.

Growing in love, growing in love with you,
Has turned my bitter life to sweet;
Those years that we were apart,
I was lost in darkness and incomplete.
I cried so heavily over you
That my tears were blue as sapphire,
How was I to know that my love would grow
Into this blazing wildfire.
True love has found its rainbow.
I'm your reality, and you're my dream come true.
Together our love will grow,

Far and beyond the starlight blue.
So come hold my hand forever,
Because I love you, deeply I do;
As long as we have faith in each other,
I know our love will see us through.

JUST FOR YOU

Look into the depths of my eyes;
See my soul with a clear view.
Absorb the warmth of my heart
As my passions slowly brew.
Feel the feelings I feel for you;
Embrace my desire.
Lose yourself in the burning bliss
And enter my heart of fire.

The fire of my love
Is like the morning sunrise:
Its light will pierce your darkness
And cast the clouds from your eyes.
My gentle ways will comfort you;
My spirit is pure love.
And the passions that dwell inside of me
Are as vast as the stars above.

Just for you…just for you…just for you,
Everything that I do or say
Comes from my heart in every way.
And all that I feel
Is ever so real
Just for you … just for you … just for you.

I'll always understand your craziness
And the anguish that you go through;
No matter how serious your problems are,
My love will stand by you.
My magic touch will ease your sorrows
As my eyes lure you into me;
My heart possesses an inner light
That will set your bonded soul free.

There is no love like my love;
My heart will always hear your cries.
And my soul will give you peace and strength
As I wipe the tears from your eyes.
I'll always show you love and affection
And give you the blood of my heart.
I'll save you from your cold depression;
When your load is heavy, I'll push your cart.

Just for you … just for you … just for you.
Everything that I do or say
Comes from my heart in every way.
And all that I feel
Is ever so real
Just for you…just for you…just for you.

Constant craving both day and night,
Sweet fervent flames;
Nothing but supreme passion for you
Flows through my veins.
When I fell in love with you, I fell forever.
Now no other woman will ever do.
My heart pulsates only true love—
A love that's just for you.

LADY OF BEAUTY

Blue fire blazes behind your lovely eyes
With such intensity, I'm mesmerized.
Two candles of infinite love—
One passion, the other desire—
Yet both burn from the same fire:
Your flaming heart.
You have changed my life forever
Ever since we've been together;
You took me into your heart
And gave me a love divine,
Stronger than the finest wine.
I'm drunk on you.

Lady of beauty, ultimate beauty,
You fill my soul with amazing bliss.
Lady of love, unconditional love,
Only your lips do I yearn to kiss.
Lady of enchantment, celestial enchantment,
My heart is a temple where my faith is true.
Lady of passion, supreme passion,
I pine for only you.
I see your beauty all the time.
Visions of you compel my mind.
I'm so absorbed into you

That I live in a constant tranquil state;
Only on you do I meditate,
Both day and night.

You're everything I ever dreamed for,
And with you in my life I'll never need for more
Because you're the very best.
You're all the beauty my eyes yearn to see;
So my angel, wrap your wings around me
And never ever let me go.
You're beautiful, so very beautiful,
That there can never be another.
You signed your name across my heart
And claimed me for your lover.
Precious, so very precious,
I'm grateful that we're together.
I cherish and adore you deeply,
And I will love you always and forever.

A DEEPER SHADE OF PINK

Created from excellence—
The highest degree—
From one empyrean whisper,
You were made just for me.
Born of love by love itself,
You're a goddess of ardent affection;
From the day you were conceived,
You oozed with perfection.

An angel of celestial sight
Made of great measure and texture,
An exposition of loveliness,
Your beauty speaks a silent gesture.
Whether it's an alluring glance
Or just your intoxicating smile,
You dominate the atmosphere
With your sweet and sultry style.

Chorus:

Sketched by the hands of infinity
And colored with exotic ink,
Your aureole of existence
Is a deeper shade of pink.
All of your character glows

A richer rose,
A lusher blush,
A darker rouge,
Inflamed pink.
I've been hypnotized by your dark, lovely eyes
Since your first seductive wink.
The essence of your enchantment
Is a deeper shade of pink.
Your creamy charisma flows
A richer rose,
A lusher blush,
A darker rouge,
Inflamed pink.

Everything about you is delicious,
My goddess of endless delights.
After tasting the nectar of your fruits,
My heart has soared to greater heights.
On the wings of passion
I've learned to truly fly
Into the realm of freedom
Where pure love is an open sky.

Your uniqueness is breathtaking.
From your head down to your feet
You're exquisitely designed inside and out,
A reflection of heaven's elite.
From the depths of your innermost recesses,
I'm saturated by the fire of your love divine,
Burning incense of ever-sweet fervor
In the chamber where our souls entwine.

Chorus:

The succulence of your kisses
Keeps my heart on constant brink

Because the pulp of your lips
Is a deeper shade of pink.
The ebullience of your passion pours
A richer rose,
A lusher blush,
A darker rouge
Inflamed pink.
You're the greatest high I've ever experienced
When our hearts are erotically in sync;
Every dose of your potent love
Is a deeper shade of pink.
The fire of your sexuality roars
A richer rose,
A lusher blush,
A darker rouge
Inflamed pink.

Only you my heart desires;
You're number one in every way.
No other woman even comes close to you,
Not even on your worst day.
You're an ultimate lady,
The finest gem ever made,
The pinkest diamond alive,
With an aura that will never fade.

Your skin is a garment of royal silk
That clothes your heavenly dwelling.
You're an incarnation of elegance;
Your radiance is overwhelming.
Full, fluorescent, and fascinating—
The pinkest lady I've ever seen.
Ever so dear to my heart and soul,
You're forever my goddess supreme.

Chorus:

Your vitality stimulates my senses
Nourishing how I feel and think.
The joy you bring into my life
Is a deeper shade of pink.
Your eminence excites
A richer rose,
A lusher blush,
A darker rouge
Inflamed pink.
Immersed by your unlimited love,
Together forever in spiritual link,
The sacred flame of our unity
Is a deeper shade of pink.
Our souls as one ignites
A richer rose,
A lusher blush,
A darker rouge
Inflamed pink.

EVERY DAY IN EVERY WAY

No matter what kind of day it is,
Rain or sunshine blue,
Whether my day is chaotic or smooth,
I'm always thinking of you.
From the moment I open my eyes,
You're the first thought on my mind;
Until I go to bed at night,
You're with me all the time.
Every day in every way,
I'm affected by you.
Every way in every day,
I'm connected to you.
I'm connected to you.

Even in my sleep,
I see your pretty face,
Taste your lips of honey,
And feel your warm embrace.
I hear your sexy whispers
As you sing me a loving tune;
And when the dream is over,
I still smell your sweet perfume.
Every day in every way,
I'm connected to you.

Every way in every day,
I'm affected by you.
I'm affected by you.

Nothing can come between us;
Our love knot is eternally secured.
And though we've been pulled, twisted, and shaken,
Our hearts have faithfully endured.
No matter how far apart we are,
Our lives never come undone.
And though at times we're distant,
Our souls remain as one.
Every day in every way,
Our love will live forever.
Every way in every day,
We're always together.
We're always together.

This world is full of anguish,
With situations beyond our control,
Yet all through the year, I hold you dear
Deep within my soul.
Feeling you, wanting you, loving you
With a passion inconceivably strong,
You're spiritually entwined to my heart,
Forever where you belong.
Every day in every way,
We're always together.
Every way in every day,
Our love will live forever.
Our love will live forever.

SEXY LADY

As bright as the morning sunrise,
You stood blissfully before my eyes:
A fine little lady with fiery hips,
Dark lovely eyes, and sugary lips.
You're the most beautiful woman I've ever seen.
I thought women like you were only a dream.
But now that I know you truly exist,
All I yearn for is to taste your kiss.
Your kisses are the fruit of my desire;
Your mouth is sweet, your tongue is fire.
I hunger for you both day and night,
Because only your love can feed me right.
You're a picture of perfect view;
I'm awed by the sight of you.
You're a fabulous work of celestial art,
And your exotic beauty has stolen my heart.
You're the most delicious woman I've ever tasted;
There's not a part of you that'll ever go wasted.
You're all the sugar and cream I need,
Because your love is the nectar that makes my heart bleed.
You're the only woman who can set my mood,
From just a whisper, to dancing in the nude,
You have captured my interest with your passionate aggression.
Now my heart and soul are forever in your possession.

WOMAN, OH WOMAN,

Woman, oh woman,
Your love is of a special blend of seeds
Planted in the soil of my heart;
You have given my life everything it needs.
Woman, oh woman,
You're a bouquet of delight,
A garden of the finest roses,
From the reddest of red to the whitest of white.
I have known many women in my life
But none of them compare to you.
Your beauty radiates
In everything you say and do.
Your heart is swollen with kindness,
Your soul possesses the sweetest of ways;
When it comes to loving, you're the very best.
No matter what the situation, your love never strays.

You're a woman of integrity;
This I know for sure.
You've proven to me countless times
That your heart is righteous and your soul is pure.
You've cared for me when I've needed you most,
And loved me through the darkest of times.
You've never forsaken me, not even once;
In the worst of storms, I've always heard your chimes.

Woman, oh woman,
You've given me more happiness than words can explain.
You've embraced my empty heart,
And ended my life of pain.
Woman, oh woman,
You've become the nectar of my life,
Ever since that beautiful day
You became my loving wife.

ANNIVERSARY SONG

A vineyard of passion,
Two hearts combined,
Blooming together,
Our souls entwined.
Year after year,
Our love ferments with time,
Becoming stronger and sweeter
Like the finest of wine.
Been through all types of weather,
Our hearts know no treason;
We survived through it all
By just going with the season.
Good or bad,
Our love stayed in place.
No matter what the tribulation,
We remained face to face.

Happy anniversary, my love, happy anniversary to you.
Another year well-worn.
Every day was lovely, beautiful, and new.
Now another year has been born.
Happy anniversary my love, happy anniversary to you.
I sing this song with joyous tears;
Another year to look forward to
As we grow older in love with the passing of years.

Falling in love with you was so easy to do.
All it took was one sweet kiss,
And into your beautiful eyes I fell,
Into a realm of overwhelming bliss.
Ever since that day, there's been no more gray.
You changed my whole life,
Filling it with your love and charm,
Erasing all my pain and strife.
Locked in love
Until death do us part,
When we said our vows,
It was straight from the heart.
From soul to soul,
Absolute love was spoken.
Sealed our oath with a kiss of fire;
Since that day, our integrity has never been broken.

Happy anniversary, my love, happy anniversary to you.
Another year well-worn.
Every day was lovely, beautiful, and new.
Now another year has been born.
Happy anniversary, my love, happy anniversary to you.
I sing this song with joyous tears;
Another year to look forward to
As we grow older in love with the passing of years.

There was no rhythm in my heart
Until you came along.
When you kissed my soul,
You brought perfect harmony to my life's song.
Everything is just crystal clear,
And your precious love is the reason why.
There's beautiful sound throughout my atmosphere.
I love you, want you, need you,
Treasure you more than anything.
I adore you, worship you, crave you,

Cherish you more than this song can ever sing.
You're more sacred to me
Than all the riches this world can give.
You and your love are all I'll ever need
To breathe freely, and to forever live.

Happy anniversary, my love, happy anniversary to you.
Another year well-worn.
Every day was lovely, beautiful, and new.
Now another year has been born.
Happy anniversary, my love, happy anniversary to you;
I sing this song with joyous tears;
Another year to look forward to
As we grow older in love with the passing of years.

LONG AFTER DEATH

When the arms of time strike death
And fate excommunicates me from life,
Don't be sad, my love,
For even in death, you're still my wife.
My love for you is eternal;
It's not bound by space or time.
Though my body will be put to rest,
My spirit cannot be confined.

The flesh lies buried in its cold, damp grave,
Rotten and relinquished,
But my soul lives forever
And its love can never be diminished.
My love for you has always been incorporeal,
Refusing to become absorbed by worldly things;
If life was unable to quarantine my love for you,
How could death ever clip my wings?

Death is incapable of abolishing my passion;
My heart is spiritually sincere.
Devotion like mine is infinitely divine,
And death can never interfere.
My soul will always remain in alliance with yours;
The love and memories will never disappear.
So don't be broken hearted when I've departed,
Because long after death, I'll still be here.

Don't become obscured by illusions;
Death has no power over me.
Its only strength is physical,
But my soul is eternally free.
Don't let your beautiful eyes age from tears
Or allow your heart to swell with woe.
Instead of mourning me for years,
Let your love for others continue to grow.

Death is part of life's cycle;
It takes us through its universal change.
Like a kaleidoscope from one phase to another,
Death carries us over to our spiritual stage.
Be one with nature and love all living things;
Feel their essence connected to you.
Look inside the beauty of all existence,
And within its depths you'll see me too.
The breath of God gave us life—
A life with an expiration date.
From the earth we came, into the earth we return;
This reality is all our fates.
I promise to love you always, forever and a day;
This vow I make is sacred and true,
So don't be frightened when I've passed away,
Because long after death, I'll still be loving you.

LET ME LOVE YOU

The past is nothing more than a ghost
Who comes to haunt you and steal your dreams,
Reminding you of what you were, or could have been.
Release what's deep inside of you,
Let go of your fears;
Forget about yesterday and all your sorrows.
Please take my heart, my gift to you.
So let me love you, let me love you.

Let's fly away together—
Far, far away,
Leaving everyone and everything behind.
Somewhere warm and tranquil,
Just you and me, heart to heart, without boundaries.
Free yourself from yourself and embrace me.
Come into my arms and feel the fire of my love.
My love is for you only;
Only you do I desire.
I cannot love another,
So let me love you, let me love you.

MAZE OF ROSES

Drearily we've walked through this maze:
You on one side, me on the other,
Just wandering through the rows of life
In search for the perfect lover.
Year after year after year,
We fell deeper into an abyss of pain,
Because every rose we ever loved
Left our hearts with a faded stain.
Deluded love,
Hidden behind their smiling eyes,
Scarred and wounded us
With a mouthful of lies.
Their lips spoke so freely of love,
Yet their hearts were full of thorns.
They pierced our love and left us to bleed,
Like two fallen pawns.
Our cries were never heard;
Silent tears poured like rain.
Loneliness just soaked our souls
As our hearts thundered in constant pain.
Frightened of this creviced path,
Never knowing which way to turn,
Yet through all the hurt and misery,
Our hunger for love continued to burn.

Roses of different colors,
Like pink, yellow, and white,
Each one with its own style,
But none of them were right.
Different in color
Yet possessing one thing the same,
For every one of them
Has caused our hearts to suffer pain.
The highest degree of excellence,
Perfection-pink,
Stayed for just a while
Then moved up a link.
The strongest rank of radiance,
Sunshine-yellow,
Yet a coward to love,
Their hearts so shallow.

The ardent flames of incandescence,
Impassioned-white,
Intensely heated fire
Always turned into a cold dark night.
After the games were played,
There was nothing left to be said,
So we took our broken hearts
And searched for the roses of red.

We're nothing in this maze
But a speck of dust, or a drop of rain.
But in the midst of it all,
To find true love, we suffered the pain.
We know the significance of a red rose:
Its essence pure, loving, and warm;
To capture what we wanted in life,
We fought our way through the storm.
Into the rows of red,
We searched for that single red rose bud

As crimson as the heart
And as sweet as blood.
With a pining for passion
And a hunger for a lifetime lover,
We turned and yearned through this maze
Until we found each other.
Face to face,
Our love spoke without a word,
Because in the depths of our eyes
True love was heard.
In one another's arms,
We felt love's bliss,
Throbbing from heart to heart,
As our lips gently kissed.

KISS OF TRUTH

When I first saw you,
My heart pounded like a wild drum
In rhythm and harmony
As my soul began to hum.
In tune with my emotions
Like I've never felt before,
You were that magic key
That opened up my door.

For a moment I thought
You were just a dream,
Just an image within my mind
Like some picture on a movie screen,
Because all my lonely life,
I've dreamt of someone just like you;
I never thought in a million years
That this dream would ever come true.

But as I moved closer to you,
I saw the love burning in your eyes;
And when I kissed your sweet lips,
I became hypnotized.
Down in my soul, I felt the warmth
Of my emotions and desire;
This kiss so deep with truth,
It set my body on fire.

From our first kiss I knew
That you were my longed-for lover;
That first kiss from you
Told me there'd be no other.
This kiss said so much;
Through our lips we felt each other's cries.
Heart to heart, soul to soul,
This kiss told no lies.

OF ONE MIND

Ever since our first kiss,
Thoughts of love have been flowing
Through my mind—
Deep emotional thoughts
Of passion, grace, and fire,
Burning, burning all the time.

In full mental awareness,
I see you always
Within my mind's eye—
Constantly pondering over you
In everything I do,
Even in the tears I cry.

Years ago within my mind,
I had a vision of you:
The picture of a perfect scene.
But now in my life
You've become my reality;
You're no longer some distant dream.

You're always on my mind.
Total concentration on you,
Number-one thought of the day,

Mental emotions so strong,
That the meditation of my love
Reflects on you in every way.

Our first kiss
Was an enlightenment
That true love was real.
It was then that I realized
The union of our love
And the beauty of its feel.

You're the fire
That burns inside my mind:
A sweet intoxicating flame.
Your essence overwhelms me.
Thoughts of loving you
Always stimulate my brain.

Since our first kiss,
The fire of our fervor
Melted our hearts together.
Absorbed into one another's thoughts
And ways of being,
We've become one mind forever.

SOUL KISS

A few years ago,
My soul was full of sorrow
And painfully alone;
In my heart no love or life;
I had no one to call my own.

I was cold, lonely, and distant,
With darkness in my eyes;
My soul lost in a realm of isolation
Where no one heard my cries.
Just me and my sadness,
A deep dreadful sigh;
Just me and my darkness,
Yearning to die.

Then you came into my life,
Out from a rainbow of dreams
With fiery love burning in your eyes.
You took away my dark, stormy clouds
And blessed me with clear blue skies.

Your love saved me from drowning
In the depths of emotional mire;
You kissed me with such passion,
Our lips became afire.

Deep down in my soul,
I burn with bliss.
This blaze of love got started
From a soul-to-soul kiss.

You've touched my spirit
And you've become part of me;
You were the spark that lit my coal.
Now we burn together
As one blazing soul.

No more dreary nights
For you or me.
It's just you and me forever,
Burning passionately.
No more tears of sorrow,
No more pain;
Our hearts have merged together
And our souls bear one name.

THE TASTE OF LOVE

It was in the kiss,
The truth of it all;
The force of our love
Broke down the wall.
Our emotions were freed
From the chain of fears;
The essence of true love
Spoke through our tears.
The taste of emotion,
Rich and sweet,
The fire on our tongues
Made us complete.
Emotional lovemaking,
Feelings of bliss,
Two hearts burning
In rapture's kiss.
I tasted the love
In the fire of your kiss;
Never ever have I felt
A hunger like this.
You've affected my body,
Heart, soul, and mind;
The force of our love
Is now combined.
Through this kiss,

All emotions were said;
From one soul to another,
We have found our rose red.
Our lips locked in a silent vow
Through the heat of our breath,
On our tongues the flavor of love
We'll savor long after death.

FUSION

Ignited feelings
Burns blue feather flames;
The intensity of love
Flows through our veins.
Our hearts now welded,
Making us one;
The bond of this love
Can never come undone.
Fiery kisses
Melted our hearts of ice
Into a blazing torch of unity,
Our love is an eternal vise.
Locked together
In the jaws of time,
The union of our souls
Is spiritually entwined.
The fusion of our love:
Joined together,
The fire in our hearts
Burns forever.
Violet flames of desire,
Our hearts a perfect blend;
In the depths of our souls,
This fervor has no end.

NAKED BUTTERFLIES

For many years, you've been my dear lover—
And what a dear lover you've been.
Ever since you came into my life,
Everything around me has become beautiful.
You're beautiful, so very beautiful.
You're the sole reason why my life has changed for the better.
The years have been great;
Every day with you is a new life,
Each hour a sweet tasting experience,
Filled with bliss and wonder.
You've given me unconditional love, devotion, and compassion.
After being touched, kissed, and loved by you,
I could never see myself in the arms of another.
My heart sighs in constant yearning for you.
My heart belongs to you. I love only you.
You're my one and only love divine.
My feelings for you are ever pure and intimate.
You're always within my heart, soul, and mind,
Sending fiery fervor throughout my veins.
You paint my world picture-perfect,
Filling my soul with those sweet, naked butterflies—
Those sweet, naked butterflies.

The essence of true love rests within the spirit;
Its force flows freely between you and me.
There's no denying this unique love,
This spiritual love of immense depth and beauty.
This love is an ultimate blessing.
This love is a miracle.
You're a miracle, a sweet dream come true,
A celestial gift from God.
From the moment I wake up next to you,
You pour burning love into my life,
Overwhelming my soul with tears of joy.
You keep my spirits riding high.
You keep my life minty and alive.
Age has not withered this precious love.
You're still the red rose of my life,
Forever fresh and in full bloom—
My eternal soulmate.
My love for you is sacred and faithful.
After all these years together, you still make my heart chime,
Filling my soul with those sweet, naked butterflies—
Those sweet, naked butterflies.

MYSTIC VIBRATIONS

My heart pulsates sonorous rhythms of empyrean love—
A love serenade composed exclusively for you;
A seductive vortex of enigmatic vibes pines deeply to be expressed.
Enter the secret auditorium of my existence,
Hear the sacred music of my concerto,
Listen to each throb pump universal love through my veins,
As a choir of blood cells sings your sweet name,
And know that I love you.

Allow my heaving heart to hypnotize you into a realm of highly harmonic
hymns of passion.
Let the delicate thunder of my soul romance you, embrace you, enrapture you.
Open yourself to the healing palpitation of my love;
Its majestic mantra will disperse your stress
And bestow a soothing mellow mood within your being.
Feel the erotic orchestration of my desire spiral itself around your aching
heart
As it builds a cocoon of nectarous kisses;
Each kiss will seep into the crevices of your old wounds
And relinquish their painful memories forever.

Lose yourself to the celestial percussions of my song.
Become one with me in its sensual symphonic sound.
Float away on the gentle murmur of my crystal stream.
Let the melodies of love cascade throughout your body.

Let their soft waves bathe your senses with blissful bubbles of clarity and
purity.
Let the sublime ripples alter your consciousness to a state of euphoria,
Uplifting your spirit to a tranquil sea of elysian dreams
Where my love for you is an endless composition of free reign—
Forever in play,
Forever in sync,
Forever alive.

FROM BLUE TO BLISS

Before you came into my life,
My world was a maelstrom of deep, dark pathos.
Its violent turbulence encircled my heart,
Leaving me dazed, diluted, and devastated.
Lost, lonely, and lacking love,
My soul ached for intimacy.
My life was blue … blue … blue—
Blue as a cold, starless night.

Once you entered my life,
The spiral of sadness expelled from my soul.
Your beautiful face changed the whole scene from bleak to bright.
Everything around me has become alive and vivid.
Your beauty surrounds me everywhere I go.
I feel your love in everything I do.
Everything I see, hear, smell, and taste is you.

Beautiful, beautiful you—
You have become the center of my being.
Because of you, my world is sacred.
Because of you, every breath I take is delicious and refreshing.
Because of you, my life has changed from blue to bliss.

IN THE REALM OF RAPTURE

The light of love pours from your eyes,
As radiant as the summer sun;
Its ardent waves have melted the icicles of my persona,
Setting my heart ablaze.
Your love has spread throughout my body like wildfire,
Flooding my veins with pulsating fever—
A temperature so intense that my skin glows with constant desire.
The flames of your fervor have lured me out of seclusion,
Out from the caves of caution,
Freeing my soul from the grips of blue devils—
No more sorrow, no more fear.
From the depths of loneliness to the depths of love—
Your love, empyreal and endless—
You have opened the gateway of your heart to me,
Welcomed me into your world
Where all is beautiful and sublime.
Embraced by red roses,
The fragrance of sweet love surrounds me.
You surround me with elysian elegance.
Intoxicated by your unsurpassable beauty,
Overwhelmed and awed by love,
I have merged myself with you completely,
Becoming one with your world.

One body, one heart, one soul—
You and me forever entwined:
Forever in unity,
Forever in love,
Forever in the realm of rapture.

INTIMATE UTTERINGS

A soft rain of tears fall freely from my heart,
Each droplet swollen with deep red fervor.
Every vein, nerve, and fiber of my flesh blazes with never-ending desire
for you.
My soul aches with fever.
The fire of absolute certainty burns rapidly throughout my being.
I'm consumed by flaming arms of love, devotion, and intimacy.
There is no antidote for my yearning.
Only the sweet kisses from your lips can comfort my restless soul.
I hunger for your lips constantly.
Your delicious kisses have unleashed my inner passions.
No one else has ever brought me such joy and happiness.
I love you ... I love you with all of my heart and all of my soul.
This kind of love comes only once in a lifetime,
When one's heart is profoundly touched by the mystical powers that only
true love can bring.

My love for you is immense, and is far beyond the space and time of this
world.
I'm completely enchanted by your beauty.
Your eyes are symphonic;
They fill my life with sweet songs,
Invigorating my soul with divine energy.
My heart is exclusively yours.
Nothing can ever dilute or taint my feelings for you.

You are my eternal red rose.
You have allowed me into your sacred garden,
Opening your petals just for me.
The secret essence of your love oozes from your heart to mine.
I inhale you deeply,
Filling my senses with all the wonders of you,
Savoring each breath I take,
Intoxicating my soul with your angelic beauty.
Because of your uniqueness, I live in a constant state of heavenly bliss.
In a moment's breath, your signature has marked my life.
In the unseen chambers of my heart your presence dwells.
Upon a tranquil lake you swim.
You are forever my swan.

I'm blind to the world when I'm with you.
There is no past, and there is no future.
Embraced by the moment, absorbed in the present,
It's your face that I see.
I'm surrounded by your beauty.
My love for you is here and now.
I live in the dimension of everlasting love.
I live for loving you.

RAINBOW

I fell in love with you
A long time ago,
And every time I think of you
My tears begin to flow.
Down my face they roll,
Like hot wax from a candle's flame,
Each tear an echo of my soul
Calling out your lovely name.
You came to me
When I was broken and alone;
You gave me your heart
And made your love be known.
You kissed my lips,
Then touched my face;
When you said you loved me,
Our hearts embraced.

I think back now with a smile
How you stopped the stormy rain,
Took away the clouds of sorrow
And eased my pain.
You filled my heart with happiness,
Joy, peace, and love;
You gave to me a brand new life
And all I ever dreamed of.

You came to me in all your beauty
Out from a heavenly rainbow;
Your heart shined through your eyes
With a warm loving glow.
You melted your way into my life,
My heart, my mind, my soul;
You were the red, red rose
That made my world whole.

IF YOU EVER TOOK FLIGHT

Just lying here in bed,
Staring at the cracked, stained ceiling,
Visions flash within my head,
Leaving me with an uneasy feeling.

The days slowly drift away,
Each second licks the face of time,
As clouds turn blue skies to gray;
I fear my absence may break your spine.

Cold sweat appears upon my brow.
I am frightened of you ever taking flight.
If you were to spread your wings now,
My life would fade into eternal night.
If you ever leave, my heart would grieve.
The most excruciating pain,
The raw reality, would pierce my brain
Like standing naked in winter rain.
There'd be no more flame, no more flame,
If you ever took flight.
If you ever leave, my soul would feel deceived.
I'd become a wretched man without a name,
Just a drunk who went insane.
My heart and soul would slowly drain,
And I would never ever be the same, be the same,
If you ever took flight.

I see myself like a fallen fruit
Just lying on the ground:
Black hearted to the root,
Everything putrid and profound.

My life would be an endless nightmare
If you ever disappeared;
There'd be no more love to share.
This is a feeling that I've always feared.

Please forgive me for having these feelings that I feel.
I just fear the thought of being brokenhearted.
Try to understand that my love for you is painfully real,
And I'd be forever lost if you ever departed.

BEFORE AND AFTER

Before you came along,
I was an unfinished song
Just waiting to be completed.
I had nowhere to belong.
Life was terribly wrong;
My heart had been depleted.
I was tired of the lies
And all the alibis.
True love was so hard to find,
So I picked up the drink
So I'd no longer think
And slowly drenched my mind.

The whiskey eased the pain
Of me having no flame
To truly call my own.
So I kissed a lot of lips,
Bumped just as many hips,
But it was better than sleeping alone.
Jumping from bed to bed,
I declared true love dead
As I lived my life off the deep end.
I just rode the tide
With no one by my side,
Embracing the bottle as my only friend.

But then there was a sudden change of weather.
Everything just got better
When you appeared like the morning sunrise.
Once we got together,
You promised to love me forever
With flames of truth blazing in your eyes.
After all these years,
You still fill life with cheers.
You've kept your promise to this day.
With your soul on fire,
And your heart of desire,
You have blessed me in every way.

Since you became my wife,
There's no more sorrow in my life.
Everything is sound and serene.
You're my lady petite,
With lips so deliciously sweet
That my world is a heavenly dream.
Before you, my life was a disaster,
But now it's happily ever after,
And you're the reason why,
Because you made me see
By proving to me
That true love can never die.

Printed in the United States
by Baker & Taylor Publisher Services